# Martha Stewart's CAKE Perfection

# Martha Stewart's CAKE *Perfection*

## 100+ Recipes for the Sweet Classic, from Simple to Stunning

*From the Kitchens of Martha Stewart*

PHOTOGRAPHS BY LENNART WEIBULL AND OTHERS

Clarkson Potter/Publishers
New York

Published in the United States by
Clarkson Potter/Publishers, an imprint
of Random House, a division of
Penguin Random House LLC, New York.
clarksonpotter.com

marthastewart.com

CLARKSON POTTER is a trademark
and POTTER with colophon is a registered
trademark of Penguin Random House LLC.

Library of Congress Control Number:
2020940872

ISBN 978-0-593-13865-6
Ebook ISBN 978-0-593-13866-3

Printed in China

Design by Michael McCormick
Cover photograph by Lennart Weibull
See page 248 for a complete list of
photography credits.

First Edition

To Jude and Truman and all young people—
who can use this book and its
delicious recipes for years to come

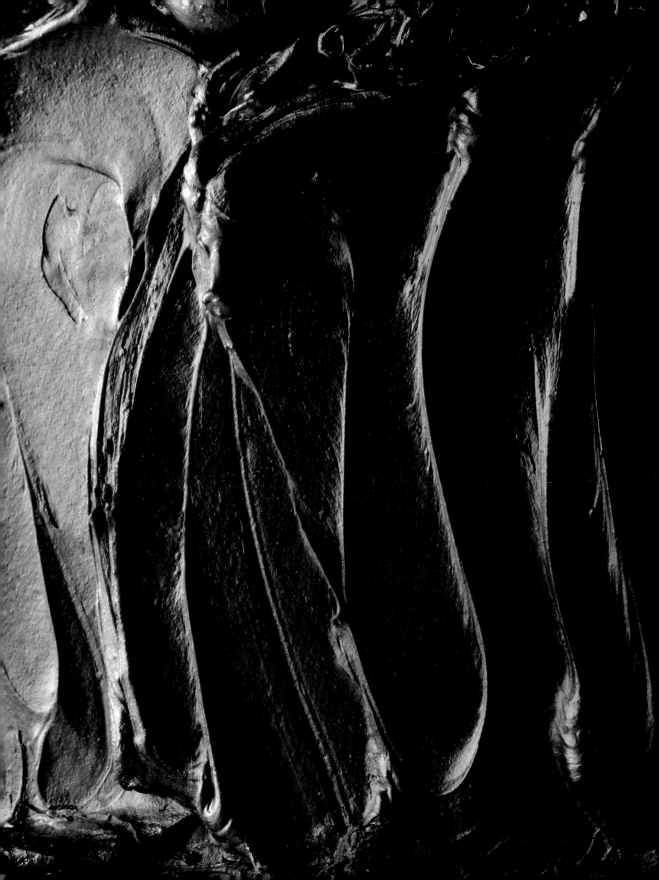

# Introduction

I recently visited my ex-son-in-law and his young family and was proudly presented with a slice of Chocolate-and-Vanilla Zebra Cake, baked by his two children. It was perfect in every way: stripes clearly delineated, frosting smooth and creamy, cake tender. I thought to myself, *If two kids under the age of twelve can execute such a seemingly complex cake, this new book, with its Show Cakes, its Layer Cakes, its Celebration Cakes, and its Cupcakes, will be a huge success.*

I, my daughter Alexis, and many of my friends and colleagues bake our own cakes—for celebrations, of course, but also for all sorts of non-events, just because we love to bake, to experiment, to be challenged. We have worked a long time perfecting the new and old favorites in this book, honing techniques so each cake will look and taste like the prototype pictured. Your cakes will be Instagram-perfect and will not last very long once that first slice is cut.

Like pie-making, where golden rules apply, cake-making needs attention to details. Have all ingredients set out, mise en place–style, so there are no surprises. You don't want to discover, as you cream the butter and sugar, that you forgot to buy the cake flour. Prepare your pans according to instructions and please pay attention to the size of the pans—inches matter! Weather also affects how the cake will turn out: Cool is better than warm, and air-conditioning, when you're frosting and decorating, can result in a finer-looking masterpiece.

I have always been a baker, creating cakes for my siblings and parents. My father loved his yellow cake with orange filling and dark chocolate buttercream, and my mother adored cakes with fruit in or on them. I have always loved anything lemon—try the Lemon Mousse Cake on page 46; it's one of my favorites. Alexis bakes *big* cakes: My fiftieth birthday cake was a mammoth coconut dessert that took one's breath away in its deliciousness and flavorfulness and size. Her children, Jude and Truman, are treated to ice cream cakes, solar system extravaganzas, and shapes emulating storybook characters and objects—all entirely natural, baked with impeccable butters and flours and creams, with the promise that each bite tastes as good as it looks.

I think you will enjoy all the cakes and the clear instructions in this book, and that you will wish there were something special to bake them for every week. Don't wait, bake anyway!

*Martha Stewart*

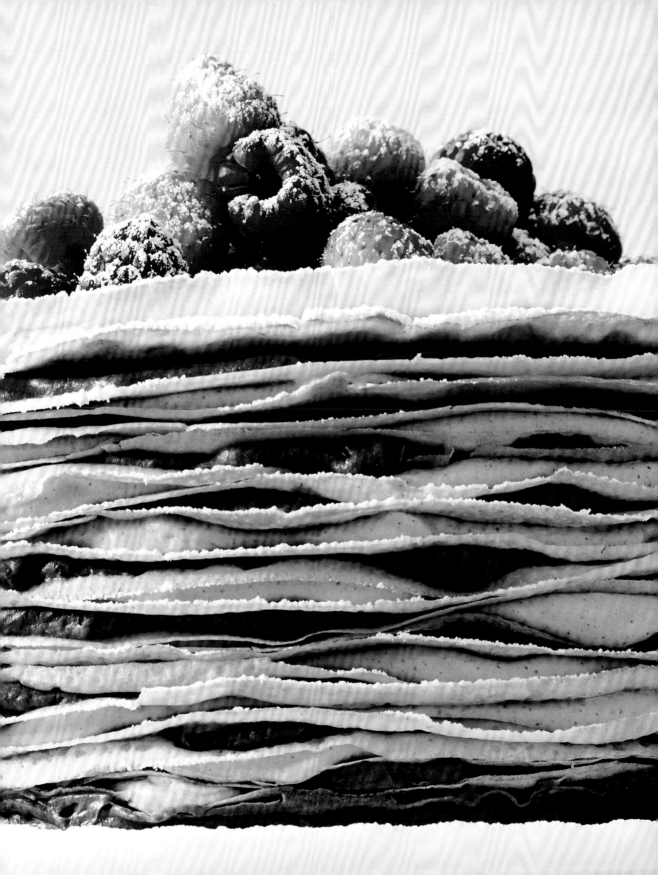

# Golden Rules

## 1. Bake a little something delicious for every occasion—

it makes even an ordinary day a bit more extra-ordinary. Practice new baking techniques, like watercolor in the Show Cakes chapter, or tuck into some classic towering tiers (Devil's Food Cake, page 78, anyone?). For weekday baking, there are everyday desserts like Rhubarb Crumb Cake (page 115) and those crowd-pleasing sheets we've come to rely on (with strawberry shortcake biscuits joining the fun on page 142). To bring out the kid in you, we included a chapter on cupcakes and took time to celebrate the holidays. Each recipe was developed to get you baking, introduce you to a new technique, flavor, or texture, or remind you of a favorite one. There's even a chapter on basic cakes and frostings, so you can mix and match as you desire.

## 2. Prep before you begin.

Before baking, read the recipe through, set the equipment nearby, and have the ingredients measured and at the right temperature. (We often call for some ingredients—such as butter and eggs—to be at room temperature. This is because they blend better than when cold—butter creams easier with sugar; egg whites whip higher; and cakes are more tender and more lofty.) As you bake, take those small extra steps that yield a truly beautiful cake: Smooth batter in pans with an offset spatula and trim the top of the baked cake layers for a flat surface.

## 3. Mind the mixing.

This book calls for two creaming methods: "Classic creaming" requires butter and sugar to be mixed together, followed by eggs, dry ingredients, and liquids. "Reverse creaming" involves beating the butter into the dry ingredients to produce an extra-tender, melt-in-your-mouth texture.

## 4. Bake in the center of the oven,

where the heat is evenly distributed, rotating cake pans 180 degrees halfway through baking. When multiple layers require two racks, utilize the upper and lower thirds. Follow the time in the recipe as a guide to judge when the cake is done; but also watch for visual cues, such as the cake pulling away from the sides of the pan, the top springing back when lightly touched, and a golden color.

## 5. Let cakes cool.

After a cake is finished baking, transfer the layers in the pans to a wire rack to cool. Generally, after 10 minutes, they are cool enough to invert: Turn out the layers onto the rack to cool completely, at least 15 minutes more. At this time, bring the frosting to room temperature for optimal dollops, swoops, and swirls.

## 6. Crumb-coat layers.

We recommend two coats of frosting for a nicely decorated cake (unless you're baking a naked cake): First create a "crumb coat," or base coat, by applying a thin layer (thin enough to still see the cake); let it chill and set before adding the remaining frosting (see page 18). A crumb coat seals in stray crumbs, allowing the second coat to appear smooth.

## 7. Decorate with aplomb.

*Martha Stewart's Cake Perfection* includes some-thing for everyone from the beginner to the prac-ticed baker, such as glazing tricks (Faux-Stone Cake, page 22) and techniques from chocolatiers (Spring Nest Cake, page 196). You can pipe all the cakes in this book with basic pastry tips, from small rounds to open and closed stars. Practice first on parchment until you're comfortable, use a flower nail (available at baking stores) to pipe flowers (and succulents), and always keep a little extra plain buttercream on hand (to fix that mistake or lighten a too-dark tinted frosting).

# Essential Ingredients

## Eggs

Egg whites act as leaveners—and are most effective when beaten, at room temperature, to stiff peaks (standing straight up when the beaters are lifted) before folding them into the batter. Meanwhile, yolks are emulsifiers, which enable fats and liquids to hold together to produce a smooth texture and rich flavor. When baking cakes, eggs generally should be brought to room temperature to blend more easily with other ingredients; take them out 30 minutes before using—if you forget, soak them in warm water for 10 minutes. Eggs are easier to separate when cold, so do so before bringing them to room temperature when the recipe calls for it.

## Flour

While most cooks stock all-purpose in the pantry, cake flour plus alternative flours like almond and semolina make honorable mention in this book. Depending on the cake, each flour has its own objective. With its higher protein content, all-purpose produces a coarser crumb, or texture, in baked goods compared to cake flour, which yields a finer, lighter texture. When using all-purpose, we prefer unbleached, as it ages naturally and holds its structure. Don't confuse cake flour with "self-rising flour"; self-rising is more closely related to all-purpose, with added salt and leaveners. The preferred method of measuring flour is to decant the dry ingredient into a widemouthed canister, whisk it to aerate, then spoon it into a measuring cup. Use a straightedge, like an offset spatula or knife, to level off the top, sweeping the excess back into the canister.

## Sugars

Stock up on granulated, brown, and confectioners' sugars. Made from refined sugarcane or sugar beet, granulated is the most common and serves as a base for most cakes. Brown is granulated sugar with molasses added—with dark brown having a higher molasses content than light brown. When measuring brown sugar, pack it tightly to eliminate air pockets or clumping. Used to make frostings and to dust desserts, confectioners' sugar is made by grinding granulated sugar to a fine powder that's then sifted and combined with cornstarch (to prevent caking). Sift confectioners' sugar before baking to remove lumps.

## Butter and oils

When it comes to baking and butter, there are two things to remember: unsalted (to better control the levels of salt) and room temperature (to blend more easily with sugar, for instance). Take butter out about 30 minutes before baking so it's soft enough to hold an indentation when you press it with your finger, but not so malleable that it melts out of shape. Some recipes in this book call for vegetable oil instead of butter to produce a finer crumb; safflower is our preferred vegetable oil.

## Salt

We call for kosher salt (we like Diamond Crystal), as it dissolves quickly in the batter. Don't substitute this coarse salt with fine or table salt, as the measurements would be quite different. A few recipes, like the Mile-High Salted-Caramel Chocolate Cake (page 98), also call for a flaky salt, such as Maldon.

## Chocolate

From bittersweet to semisweet, chocolate is featured in cake layers, frostings, ganaches, and fillings. The higher the percentage of cacao (the chocolate liquor), the richer the taste—we favor *at least* 61% cacao. Chocolate can be used alone or with cocoa powder. Generally, we prefer unsweetened Dutch-process cocoa powder over natural, because it's less acidic and produces a darker, smoother-tasting chocolate.

# Essential Tools

## Cake pans

The recipes in this book utilize a variety of round pans, ranging from 7 to 10 inches. Rimmed baking sheets also come into play, and a 9-by-13-by-2-inch pan for sheet cakes and a 10-by-15-by-1-inch jelly pan (a very shallow baking pan) for sponge-type cakes. And get out a standard muffin pan for the cupcake chapter. Additional useful pans: a springform, skillet, and loaf.

## Flexible spatula

This comes in handy for stirring melted chocolate, frosting cakes, and getting every delicious drop out of a bowl. Silicone spatulas tend to be more resistant to heat than rubber.

## Offset spatulas

The angled design of these tools proves invaluable for smoothing batters, frosting cakes, transferring piping details, and myriad other baking tasks.

## Parchment paper

An indispensable pantry item for lining pans and practicing piping techniques. Tuck strips of parchment beneath cakes when you decorate.

## Measuring cups

Use a graduated set to measure dry ingredients, such as flours, and a clear one for liquids, like oils and milk.

## Bench scraper

Made of stainless steel or plastic, a bench scraper can be used for smoothing a crumb coat, to transfer cake layers, and to clean off surfaces.

## Pastry bags and piping tips

Pastry bags and tips are sold both separately and together as sets. Purchase a set that meets your basic needs, then add on as your skills progress; most tips come in more than one size.

## Serrated knife

This is your go-to tool for chopping chocolate and nuts. The jagged edges will level a cake and split a layer in half without tearing; choose one that is long enough to extend all the way through the cake.

## Oven thermometer

Keep one in your oven to make sure the temperature is accurate, and adjust accordingly.

## Pastry brush

Stock up with a few, in various sizes, for buttering pans, brushing away crumbs before frosting, and brushing on glaze or melted chocolate.

## Wooden skewers

Skewers, toothpicks, dowels: insert a skewer (or cake tester) into a cake to see if it's done. Use toothpicks to tint icing with food coloring and to mark where to split a cake. Dowels will ensure layers stand at attention.

## Wire rack

Most of our recipes require the pans to cool on a wire rack. A raised rack will allow air to circulate beneath the pans as they cool.

## Cake boards

Anchor a cake layer to the precut cardboard round with a dab of buttercream, making it easier to transfer a layer cake both from the turntable to the refrigerator while you frost it and to the table for serving. You can also use it to move individual cake layers. Look for them at cake stores or online.

## Rotating turntable

This allows you to spin the cake as you're decorating. If you don't have a rotating turntable, use a cake stand or place a plate on an inverted bowl (see cover).

# Basic Frosting Techniques

## 1. Trim the cake:

After they have baked and cooled in the pans, turn the cake layers out onto a rack, top-sides up, to cool completely. With a long serrated knife, trim the top off each layer to make a level (flat) surface. Using a pastry brush, remove any stray crumbs.

## 2. Spread the filling:

Line the edges of a cake stand or plate with strips of parchment to keep the surface tidy. Transfer a cake layer, trimmed-side up, to the stand. Using a small offset spatula, evenly cover the top of the first layer with 1 to 1½ cups filling: Place the frosting in the center of the cake layer; then spread the filling toward the edges. Use the offset spatula to make the filling layer smooth and even, so the cake will stack straight.

## 3. Crumb-coat:

Place the second cake layer, trimmed-side down, on top of the filling; press gently to make it level. To avoid getting crumbs in the frosting, apply a thin base coat to seal them in: With a small offset spatula, spread 1 to 1½ cups buttercream, meringue, or whatever frosting you're using over the entire cake. Refrigerate for 15 minutes to 30 minutes.

## 4. Frost and smooth the cake:

Using a large offset spatula, generously coat the chilled cake with about 2½ cups buttercream, frosting the top of cake first. Hold the spatula at a 45-degree angle against the cake and slowly rotate the turntable. Next, you'll either create a desired decorative look or smooth the sides of the cake. If smoothing, use a bench scraper. Hold the scraper perpendicular to the cake, with one edge resting on the turntable, and slowly rotate the turntable. Touch up areas of the cake with a small offset spatula, then gently remove the parchment strips. Refrigerate the cake for 30 minutes, or as the recipe directs.

# 1
# Show Cakes

*These beauties are all about fabulous
techniques: piped rosettes, glossy glazes, vertical layers,
swoops, swirls, and splatters.
Each of these cakes knows how to put on a show.*

# Faux-Stone Cake

*The key to this high-gloss showstopper is combining different shades of white chocolate glaze: Pour it over the cake (we baked the Basic Chocolate, on page 229) at the right temperature so it dries to a mirror-like finish. We chose three shades of blue here, but you could use a different color combination to replicate your favorite stone.*

---

Two 9-inch cakes
(see Mix-and-Match
Cakes, page 226)

Frosting (see Mix-and-Match
Frostings, page 237)

3 envelopes (¼ ounce
each) unflavored gelatin

½ cup cold water

1½ cups sugar

7 ounces sweetened
condensed milk

Pinch of kosher salt

12 ounces white chocolate,
coarsely chopped

Gel-paste food
coloring in 3 shades of blue,
such as Wedgwood,
Sky Blue, and Royal Blue

**1.** With a serrated knife, trim tops of cake layers to level. Place a layer, bottom-side down, on a wire rack set over a parchment-lined rimmed baking sheet. Spread ¼ cup frosting evenly over cake layer. Place second layer, bottom-side up, on top. Spread a thin layer of frosting over cake to form a crumb coat. Chill in freezer until cold and firm, about 2 hours.

**2.** In a small bowl, sprinkle gelatin over cold water. Let stand until softened, about 5 minutes. Meanwhile, combine sugar, condensed milk, salt, and ½ cup water in a small saucepan; bring to a gentle simmer over low heat. Remove from heat; stir in gelatin mixture until dissolved (mixture should feel smooth when rubbed between your fingers).

**3.** Place white chocolate in a medium bowl. Pour milk mixture over chocolate and let stand 5 minutes; mix with a spatula until combined. Using an immersion blender, blend until mixture is smooth. Using a fine-mesh sieve, strain mixture into a large measuring cup.

**4.** Divide mixture into 4 small bowls. Add gel, a drop at a time, to 3 bowls until desired shades are reached. Pour all 4 back into measuring cup (do not mix). Let glaze cool until it registers 95°F on a candy thermometer.

**5.** Meanwhile, place a wire rack on a parchment-lined rimmed baking sheet. Transfer chilled cake to rack, elevating it on a smaller-size cake pan or sturdy bowl, to allow glaze to drip down and cover sides neatly.

**6.** Using a back-and-forth motion, pour glaze over cake. (Gently shake baking sheet and tap it on a counter, if necessary, to ensure that glaze covers cake.) Using a skewer or toothpick, pop any air bubbles. Let glaze set at least 30 minutes before serving. To serve, dip a knife in hot water, wipe it dry, and cut cake into wedges.

**DECORATING TIP**

Chill the cake for about 2 hours before glazing to help the pattern set.

# S'mores Cake

MAKES ONE 8-INCH LAYER CAKE

*The classic campfire flavor combination of chocolate, graham crackers,
and marshmallow gets a bit more sophisticated—with chocolate ganache and Swiss
meringue, which is like marshmallow, but lighter and a little less sweet.*

---

## FOR THE CAKE

2 sticks (1 cup) unsalted butter, room temperature, plus more for pans

2 cups unbleached all-purpose flour, plus more for pans

1 cup graham cracker crumbs

1 tablespoon baking powder

1 teaspoon kosher salt

1 teaspoon ground cinnamon

1½ cups granulated sugar

½ cup packed dark-brown sugar

3 large eggs, room temperature

2 teaspoons vanilla extract

1½ cups whole milk

Chocolate Ganache Filling (page 241)

## FOR THE "MARSHMALLOW" TOPPING

1½ cups granulated sugar

1½ cups light corn syrup

¼ teaspoon kosher salt

4 large egg whites, room temperature

1 tablespoon vanilla extract

---

**1. Make the cake:** Preheat oven to 350°F. Butter two 8-inch round cake pans. Line bottom with parchment; butter parchment. Dust with flour, tapping out any excess. In a medium bowl, whisk together flour, graham cracker crumbs, baking powder, salt, and cinnamon. With an electric mixer, beat butter and both sugars on medium-high until light and fluffy, about 3 minutes, scraping down sides of bowl as needed. Add eggs, one at a time, beating well. Stir in vanilla. In a large bowl, with mixer on low, add flour mixture in three batches, alternating with milk. Divide batter evenly between prepared pans, smoothing tops with an offset spatula. Bake until golden brown, about 45 minutes. Transfer pans to a wire rack to cool 10 minutes. Turn out cakes onto rack to cool completely.

**2. Make the marshmallow topping:** In a small saucepan, heat granulated sugar, corn syrup, ½ cup water, and the salt over high heat without stirring until mixture registers 240°F on a candy thermometer. With an electric mixer, whisk egg whites on medium speed until foamy. Increase speed to medium-high until soft peaks form, about 2 minutes. Reduce speed to low and drizzle hot sugar syrup down side of bowl in a slow, steady stream. Whip mixture until stiff and glossy, about 7 minutes. Blend in vanilla and 2 tablespoons water. Transfer to a pastry bag fitted with a medium star tip.

**3.** With a serrated knife, trim tops of cake layers to level; split each horizontally to form 4 layers. Place a trimmed cake layer on a cake stand. Place ganache in a pastry bag fitted with a ¼-inch round tip. Pipe a ring of ganache around perimeter and fill, spreading with a small offset spatula. Chill for 5 minutes. Repeat ganache process on two additional layers. Remove bottom layer from refrigerator. Pipe a ring of marshmallow topping over ganache and fill, spreading with an offset spatula. Place second cake layer on top. Repeat with additional layers; top with final layer. Insert two dowels in center of cake, trimmed just shorter than top of cake. Pipe remaining marshmallow topping in peaks around top of cake: Holding pastry bag at a 90-degree angle, squeeze and release halfway into each peak. Use a kitchen torch to toast frosting until evenly browned.

# Citrus Cake with Edible Blossoms

## MAKES ONE 8-INCH LAYER CAKE

*This stunner is bursting with citrusy flavor—lemony cake and light,
lime-mousse filling—and is wrapped in a cloud of Italian meringue buttercream. Start with
a few charming edible blossoms, a scattering of sugar pearls, maybe
a few meringues and decorate at will—turning any event into a fanciful occasion.*

---

2½ sticks (1¼ cups) unsalted butter, room temperature, plus more for pans

3¾ cups unbleached all-purpose flour, plus more for pans

3¼ teaspoons baking powder

¼ teaspoon baking soda

2 teaspoons kosher salt

2½ cups sugar

2 teaspoons finely grated lemon zest plus ¼ cup fresh juice

5 large eggs, room temperature

1½ cups buttermilk, room temperature

Citrus Mousse Filling (page 231)

4 cups Italian Meringue Buttercream (page 238) or Whipped Cream (page 242)

Edible flowers, store-bought meringues, and sugar pearls, for decorating

**1.** Preheat oven to 325°F. Butter two 8-by-2-inch round cake pans. Line bottom with parchment; butter parchment. Dust with flour, tapping out any excess. In a medium bowl, whisk together flour, baking powder, baking soda, and salt until combined.

**2.** In a large bowl, with an electric mixer, beat butter with sugar and zest on medium-high until light and fluffy. Add eggs, one at a time, beating well after each addition and scraping down sides of bowl as needed. Beat in lemon juice. With mixer on low, add flour mixture in three batches, alternating with buttermilk and beginning and ending with flour.

**3.** Divide batter evenly between prepared pans, smoothing tops with an offset spatula. Bake, rotating pans halfway through, until light golden and tops spring back when lightly touched, about 1 hour 10 minutes. Transfer pans to a wire rack to cool 10 minutes. Turn out cakes onto rack to cool completely. (Cakes can be made to this point and refrigerated, well wrapped in plastic, up to 1 day.)

**4.** With a serrated knife, trim tops of cake layers to level; split each horizontally into 3 equal layers to form a total of 6 layers. Line an 8-inch cake pan with 2 parchment strips, leaving a 3-inch overhang on all sides.

**5.** Assemble cake in prepared pan: Place a cake layer in pan, bottom-side down. Spread 1 cup citrus mousse evenly over it; top with a second cake layer, bottom-side down. Repeat, spreading 1 cup citrus mousse between each layer. Finish with a cake layer, bottom-side up. Refrigerate, covered in plastic, at least 1 hour and up to overnight.

**6.** Using parchment overhang, remove cake from pan to a cake plate. Spread 1 cup buttercream evenly over top and sides to create a crumb coat. Refrigerate 15 minutes. Spread remaining 3 cups buttercream evenly over top and sides. Decorate as desired.

**DECORATING TIP**
Begin applying
the decorations at one
top corner of the
cake and working
around the perimeter,
leaving some
space unadorned.

**BAKING TIP**

The baking time for meringues will
vary depending on the kitchen's humidity.
Bake them until they pull off the
parchment easily.

# Coconut-and–Strawberry Ice Cream Meringues

**MAKES 12**

*Crisp-chewy meringues meet cool, creamy strawberry ice cream
to transform the confection into a blushing cake-like dessert. The light-as-air disks,
tinted the palest shade of pink, are made by swirling meringues
onto parchment, sprinkling them with coconut, and baking until just dry.*

---

1½ cups sugar

6 large egg whites,
room temperature

Pinch of kosher salt

Gel–paste food coloring
in red, such as Tulip Red

¼ cup finely shredded
unsweetened coconut

Store–bought strawberry
ice cream, softened

6 strawberries,
halved, for garnish

**1.** Preheat oven to 175°F. Line 4 baking sheets with parchment. Trace nine 3½-inch circles onto each sheet. Turn parchment traced-sides down.

**2.** In a heatproof bowl set over (not in) a pan of simmering water, heat sugar, egg whites, and salt, whisking constantly, until warm to the touch and sugar is dissolved, about 3 minutes. Remove bowl from heat. With an electric mixer on medium-high speed, whisk until stiff, glossy peaks form, about 4 minutes. Blend in gel to reach desired shade (we used 1 drop).

**3.** Dab a bit of meringue under corners of parchment to hold it in place. Spread 3 heaping tablespoons meringue within edges of each traced circle. Sprinkle 1 teaspoon coconut each over 12 of the rounds.

**4.** Bake until meringues are dry but not taking on any color and can be easily pulled off parchment, 1½ to 2 hours. Transfer sheets to a wire rack to cool completely.

**5.** Using a small offset spatula, form ¼-cup scoops of softened ice cream into 3-inch disks. Place an ice-cream disk on a plain meringue. Top with a second plain meringue and a second ice-cream disk, then end with a coconut-sprinkled round. Transfer to a parchment-lined rimmed baking sheet. Repeat with remaining meringues and ice cream. Freeze, at least 5 hours and up to 1 day. Top each with a halved strawberry before serving.

# Lemon Honey Cake

**MAKES ONE 8-INCH LAYER CAKE**

*This rustic cake is infused with honey, lemon, and a hint of ground cardamom.
Four layers—made tender with oil, milk, honey, and brown sugar—are brushed with more
honey, then spread with a satiny-smooth filling that's a cross between lemon
curd and cream cheese frosting. To take it to the next level, we topped it with honeycomb.*

---

### FOR THE CAKE

Vegetable cooking spray

1¾ cups unbleached
all-purpose flour

¾ teaspoon baking powder

½ teaspoon baking soda

1 teaspoon kosher salt

½ teaspoon ground cardamom

1 cup honey

½ cup whole milk

½ cup safflower oil

2 large eggs,
room temperature

¾ packed light-brown sugar

1 teaspoon finely
grated lemon zest

Honeycomb piece,
for serving (optional)

### FOR THE CURD

2 large eggs plus 3 large yolks

¾ cup granulated sugar

½ cup fresh lemon juice
(from 2 to 3 lemons)

8 ounces cream cheese, cut
into cubes, room temperature

**1. Make the cake:** Preheat oven to 325°F. Coat two 8-inch round cake pans with cooking spray. Line with parchment; spray parchment. In a medium bowl, whisk together flour, baking powder, baking soda, salt, and cardamom. In another bowl, whisk together ½ cup honey, the milk, and oil. With an electric mixer, whisk together eggs, brown sugar, and zest on high speed until thickened, about 3 minutes. Reduce speed to medium and slowly add honey mixture; beat to combine, about 1 minute. Reduce speed to low, gradually add flour mixture, and beat until combined.

**2.** Divide batter evenly between prepared pans, smoothing tops with an offset spatula. Bake until tops spring back and edges start to pull away from sides of pan, about 25 minutes. Transfer pans to a wire rack to cool 20 minutes. Turn out cakes onto rack to cool completely.

**3. Make the curd:** In a medium saucepan, combine eggs, yolks, granulated sugar, and lemon juice over high heat and cook, whisking constantly, until thickened, about 2 minutes. Remove from heat; whisk in cream cheese, one piece at a time. Strain mixture through a fine-mesh sieve into a medium bowl, pressing on solids to extract liquid (about 2 cups); discard solids. Cover curd with plastic wrap, pressing it directly onto surface. Refrigerate until cold, at least 2 hours and up to 1 day.

**4. For assembly:** Using a serrated knife, trim tops of cakes to level; split each cake in half horizontally to form a total of 4 layers. Place a cake bottom on a cake stand. Spread 2 tablespoons honey over top. Spread ½ cup curd over top, stopping slightly short of edges; top with a cake layer, cut-side up. Spread with 2 tablespoons honey and another ½ cup curd. Repeat with second cake bottom, 2 more tablespoons honey, and ½ cup curd. Spread cut side of final cake layer with remaining 2 tablespoons honey, then place on top of assembled cake, top-side up. Spread top with remaining ½ cup curd, swirling as desired. Refrigerate at least 1 hour and up to 6 hours before serving, topped with honeycomb, if using.

# German Chocolate Bundt Cake

### SERVES 10 TO 12

*Dressed up as a Bundt and drizzled with sleek chocolate glaze, the German chocolate cake's signature coconut-pecan topping is tucked inside. No need to track down buttermilk; simply combine milk and vinegar and let stand five minutes.*

---

**FOR THE CAKE**

1 cup pecans

1½ sticks (¾ cup) unsalted butter, room temperature, plus more for pan

2 cups plus 2 tablespoons unbleached all-purpose flour, plus more for pan

1¼ cups unsweetened finely shredded coconut

1 cup cream of coconut (from one 15-ounce can)

¾ cup whole milk, room temperature

2 tablespoons distilled white vinegar

3 tablespoons Dutch-process cocoa powder

1 teaspoon baking soda

1¼ teaspoons kosher salt

1¼ cups sugar

3 large eggs, room temperature

2 teaspoons vanilla extract

5 ounces semisweet chocolate, melted and cooled slightly

**FOR THE GLAZE**

5 ounces semisweet chocolate, chopped (1 cup)

⅔ cup heavy cream

**1. Make the cake:** Preheat oven to 350°F. Spread pecans in a single layer on a rimmed baking sheet; toast until darkened slightly and fragrant, 10 to 12 minutes. Let cool slightly, then finely chop.

**2.** Generously brush a 10- to 15-cup Bundt pan with butter; dust with flour, tapping out excess. In a saucepan, stir together shredded coconut, cream of coconut, and 2 tablespoons flour. Bring to a boil, then reduce heat to medium and boil 30 seconds. Remove from heat, stir in pecans, and let cool completely. Meanwhile, stir together milk and vinegar; let stand until curdled, about 5 minutes.

**3.** In a medium bowl, whisk remaining 2 cups flour, the cocoa, baking soda, and salt. With an electric mixer, beat butter with sugar on medium-high speed in a large bowl until pale and fluffy, 2 to 3 minutes. Add eggs, one at a time, beating well. Beat in vanilla. Reduce speed to low and beat in flour mixture in three additions, alternating with milk mixture, and beginning and ending with flour, just until combined. Beat in chocolate.

**4.** Pour batter into prepared pan, smoothing top with an offset spatula. Using a small ice cream scoop, dollop coconut mixture evenly on top of batter in a ring, leaving a ½-inch border around sides and center. (It will sink down into the batter as the cake bakes.)

**5.** Bake until a wooden skewer inserted in center of cake layer comes out clean, 45 to 50 minutes. Transfer to a wire rack to cool 20 minutes. Turn out cake onto rack to cool completely.

**6. Make the glaze:** Place chocolate in a heatproof bowl. In a small saucepan, bring heavy cream to a simmer. Pour over chocolate and let stand 5 minutes. Gently stir until smooth. Let stand until thickened slightly but still warm and thin enough to pour, about 5 minutes. Pour evenly over top of cake; let stand until set, about 30 minutes. Transfer to a cake stand or plate; slice and serve. (Glazed cake can be stored, loosely covered with parchment-lined foil, at room temperature for up to 2 days.)

# Strawberry Ombré Cake
# with Rose-Gold Leaf

**MAKES ONE 8-INCH LAYER CAKE**

*Any guest of honor would be knocked out by this glitzy, pink-and-rose-gold ombré production: Five different shades of vanilla cake are layered with strawberry jam and buttercream—then all dressed up with rose gold. We created a crescent moon design with the gold leaf, but you can also simply cover the top rim of the cake.*

2 sticks (1 cup) unsalted butter, cut into tablespoons, room temperature, plus more for pan

3 cups cake flour (not self–rising), plus more for pan

1¼ cups whole milk

4 large eggs, room temperature

1 teaspoon vanilla extract

1¾ cups sugar

1 tablespoon baking powder

1 teaspoon kosher salt

Gel–paste food coloring in pink, such as Deep Pink

½ cup seedless strawberry jam

Zest and juice of ½ lemon

2 recipes Swiss Meringue Buttercream (page 237)

Edible–grade rose–gold leaf

**1.** Preheat oven to 350°F with racks in upper and lower thirds. Butter five 8-inch round cake pans. Line each with parchment; butter parchment. Dust with flour, tapping out any excess. In a medium bowl, whisk together milk, eggs, and vanilla.

**2.** In a large bowl, with an electric mixer, beat flour, sugar, baking powder, and salt on low speed until well combined. Continue beating while gradually adding butter until mixture is crumbly, about 3 minutes.

**3.** Slowly add half the milk mixture; increase speed to medium and beat until fluffy, about 2 minutes. Slowly add remaining milk mixture, scraping down sides of bowl as needed. Beat until incorporated, about 1 minute more. Divide batter between 5 bowls (about a heaping cup per bowl).

**4.** Tint 4 batters with pink gel, gradually adding more to each one to create shades. Transfer batters to prepared pans, spreading to edges and smoothing tops with a small offset spatula. Tap pans on counter. Bake until a cake tester comes out clean, about 15 minutes. Transfer pans to a wire rack to cool completely; then turn out cakes.

**5.** Meanwhile, in a small saucepan, heat jam with lemon zest and juice over low until warm. In a separate bowl, add gel, a drop at a time, to buttercream, mixing to desired shade of light pink.

**6.** Place darkest layer on an 8-inch cake round. Using a pastry brush, brush cake with a thin layer of jam mixture, then spread 1 cup buttercream evenly with an offset spatula. Repeat process for 4 more layers, stacking from darkest to lightest. Spread a thin layer of frosting over cake to form a crumb coat; refrigerate until firm, about 30 minutes. Spread top and sides of cake evenly with about a ½-inch thickness of buttercream, smoothing sides with an offset spatula or bench scraper. Refrigerate until chilled, about 20 minutes. Using a dry food-safe paintbrush, tear off pieces of rose-gold leaf and place onto cake, decorating as desired.

**DECORATING TIP**

Use a dry
paintbrush, not
your fingers,
when tearing and
placing the
rose-gold leaf.

**BAKING TIP**

Fresh ricotta is a
must for this recipe.
It has a lightly sweet,
floral flavor that
is incomparable.
You can find fresh
ricotta in many large
supermarkets in
the specialty cheese
section, or make it
yourself (page 245).

# Pistachio Cannoli Cake

MAKES ONE 8-INCH CAKE

*In this homage to the iconic Sicilian pastries—typically ricotta-stuffed and studded with dried fruit, nuts, or chocolate—we keep the filling more traditional but swap out the standard tube-shaped shells for cake layers. The buttery rounds get flavored with orange-flower water, brushed with melted chocolate, and dotted with crushed pistachios.*

### FOR THE CAKE

1 stick (½ cup) plus 2 tablespoons unsalted butter, room temperature, plus more for pans

1½ cups unbleached all-purpose flour, plus more

½ cup plus 3 tablespoons shelled unsalted pistachios

1½ teaspoons baking powder

¼ teaspoon baking soda

1 teaspoon kosher salt

1 cup granulated sugar

¼ teaspoon orange-flower water (optional)

2 large eggs plus 2 large yolks, room temperature

1 cup sour cream

### FOR THE FILLING

2¾ cups fresh ricotta

¾ cup heavy cream

¼ teaspoon kosher salt

1 teaspoon vanilla extract

¼ teaspoon ground cinnamon

¾ cup confectioners' sugar, plus more for serving

4 ounces semisweet chocolate, coarsely chopped (¾ cup), plus 2½ ounces more, melted (½ cup)

4 ounces candied orange peel, cut into a ¼-inch dice

**1. Make the cake:** Preheat oven to 350°F. Butter two 8-by-2-inch round cake pans. Line pans with parchment; butter parchment. Dust with flour, tapping out excess. In a food processor, finely grind pistachios; reserve ¼ cup. Add flour, baking powder, baking soda, and salt and pulse to combine. With an electric mixer, beat butter with granulated sugar on medium-high speed until light and fluffy, about 2 minutes. Add orange-flower water, if using, and beat to combine. Beat in eggs and yolks, one at a time, combining after each addition and scraping down bowl as needed. Add pistachio mixture in three batches, alternating with sour cream and beginning and ending with pistachio mixture.

**2.** Divide batter evenly between cake pans, smoothing tops with an offset spatula. Bake, rotating pans once, until tops spring back when lightly touched, 30 to 35 minutes. Transfer pans to a wire rack to cool 10 minutes. Turn cakes out onto rack to cool completely, 1 hour. Wrap in plastic and refrigerate at least 1 hour and up to overnight.

**3. Make the filling:** In a food processor, pulse ricotta and cream until smooth. Add salt, vanilla, cinnamon, and confectioners' sugar; process to combine. Transfer mixture to a bowl and stir in chopped chocolate and orange peel. Chill in an airtight container at least 1 hour and up to 2 days.

**4.** With a serrated knife, trim tops of cakes to level; split each cake horizontally into 2 layers. Stack on a cardboard cake round or a plate; brush edges with melted chocolate; then pat some of reserved ground pistachios onto chocolate. Refrigerate in a single layer until set, 10 minutes. Place one cake layer on a cake stand, bottom-side down, and spread 1½ cups filling evenly over top; then place second layer on top. Repeat with remaining filling and cakes, finishing with a cake layer, bottom-side up. Refrigerate at least 1 hour and up to overnight. Sprinkle with confectioners' sugar and remaining reserved ground pistachios.

# Triple-Chocolate Ice Cream Cake

**MAKES ONE 9-INCH CAKE**

*Go vertical with the layers of this graphic dessert. It all starts with two cakes: one baked in a jelly-roll pan, the other in a round. You coat the rectangular cake in white chocolate ganache and slice it into strips before assembling and filling with ice cream. Crown it with whipped cream and milk chocolate shavings, and wait for the* How did you do that?

Unsalted butter, room temperature, for pans

¾ cup unsweetened Dutch-process cocoa powder, plus more for pans

1½ cups unbleached all-purpose flour

1½ cups sugar

1½ teaspoons baking soda

¾ teaspoon baking powder

¾ teaspoon kosher salt

2 large eggs, room temperature

¾ cup buttermilk, room temperature

3 tablespoons safflower oil

1 teaspoon vanilla extract

¾ cup warm water

White Chocolate Ganache (page 241)

2 quarts chocolate ice cream, softened

Whipped Cream (page 242), for serving

Milk chocolate curls (page 245), for serving

**1.** Preheat oven to 350°F. Butter one 9-inch round cake pan. Line with parchment; butter parchment. Dust with cocoa, tapping out any excess. Repeat process with a 15½-by-10½ inch jelly-roll pan. In a large bowl, with an electric mixer, beat cocoa, flour, sugar, baking soda, baking powder, and salt on low speed until just combined. Add eggs, buttermilk, oil, and vanilla and mix to combine. Add warm water, increase speed to medium, and beat until smooth, about 3 minutes.

**2.** Place 1 cup batter in prepared 9-inch round cake pan and remaining batter in jelly-roll pan, spreading batter evenly and smoothing tops with an offset spatula. Bake until set and a cake tester comes out clean, 12 to 14 minutes. Transfer pans to a wire rack to cool 15 minutes. Turn out cakes onto rack to cool completely.

**3.** Trim edges of rectangular cake to make even. Top with ganache, spreading it evenly to the edges. Using a ruler, divide cake into quarters, and stack them on top of one another, pressing down gently to adhere layers. Wrap in plastic and chill for 30 minutes. Using a ruler, cut cake lengthwise into strips 1-inch wide, and then cut each strip in half (3½ to 4 inches tall).

**4.** Set 9-inch cake into a 10-inch springform pan. Place cake strips around cake's perimeter, flush with the edge of the pan. Fill interior of pan with ice cream, wrap in plastic, and freeze overnight. Just before serving, remove from pan and top with whipped cream. Garnish with chocolate curls.

**BAKING TIP**

Chop the white chocolate for the ganache in small pieces so that it melts evenly. If the chunks are too large, the outside surface will melt before the center begins to soften, and the melted portion will stay hot too long, ruining the ganache.

# Watercolor Cake

MAKES ONE 8-INCH LAYER CAKE

*Bring your best impressionist impression to the table with this artful marble layer cake, covered with buttercream in the same shades as the interior. The watercolor effect is achieved by blending two tinted buttercreams with plain— just enough to blur their borders, like the artwork that inspired the cake.*

3 sticks (1½ cups) unsalted butter, room temperature, plus more for pans

4½ cups cake flour (not self–rising), plus more for pans

1½ tablespoons baking powder

¾ teaspoon kosher salt

2 cups sugar

6 large eggs, room temperature

1 tablespoon vanilla extract

1½ cups whole milk

¼ cup safflower oil

Gel-paste food coloring in pink and lavender

2 recipes Swiss Meringue Buttercream (page 237)

**1.** Preheat oven to 350°F. Butter three 8-inch round cake pans. Line with parchment; butter parchment. Dust with flour, tapping out any excess. In a large bowl, whisk together flour, baking powder, and salt. With an electric mixer, beat butter and sugar on medium-high speed until light and fluffy, about 5 minutes. Add eggs, one at a time, beating until just combined and scraping down sides of bowl as needed. Mix in vanilla. Add flour mixture in three batches, alternating with milk and oil, and beginning and ending with flour.

**2.** Divide batter among 3 bowls. Using gel, tint 2 batters to desired shades, leaving third batter plain (this will be your base batter). Divide plain batter among prepared cake pans; then evenly distribute tinted batters by the spoonful over the plain base batter. Marble batter: Insert a butter knife or skewer vertically to bottom of pan, then swirl together batters.

**3.** Bake until just golden and a cake tester comes out clean, 30 to 35 minutes. Transfer pans to a wire rack to cool 10 minutes. Turn out cakes onto rack to cool completely. With a serrated knife, trim tops of cakes to level.

**4.** Reserve 1 generous cup Swiss meringue buttercream. Anchor a cake layer, bottom-side down, on a cake board with a dab of buttercream. Spread evenly with 1¼ cups buttercream. Repeat, ending with the final cake layer, bottom-side up. Spread a thin layer of frosting over cake to form a crumb coat; refrigerate until firm, about 30 minutes.

**5.** Divide reserved buttercream among 3 bowls. Tint to desired shades, using same gel used in cake batter. Place cake on a cake stand and frost with remaining plain buttercream. Using a small offset spatula, dab tinted buttercreams sparingly around cake (you may not need all the tinted buttercream). Using a large offset spatula or a bench scraper, set an edge against the side of the cake and, spinning cake stand evenly, smooth frosting, creating a watercolor effect as the tinted buttercreams blend together with the plain.

# Cranberry Curd and Citrus Pavlova

### SERVES 8 TO 10

*A tart cranberry-orange curd offsets the sweetness of the crisp meringue shell.
For the best volume on the meringue, use fresh eggs and beat the whites
at room temperature. Serve the pavlova with a billow of whipped cream, segments of
your favorite citrus, and, if you can get them, a smattering of cape gooseberries.*

---

**FOR THE PAVLOVA**

1¼ cups sugar

4 teaspoons cornstarch

5 large egg whites,
room temperature (reserve
2 yolks for Cranberry Curd)

1 teaspoon fresh lemon juice

¼ teaspoon kosher salt

2½ cups mixed sweet citrus,
such as clementine; mandarin;
navel, Cara Cara, and blood
orange; and small ruby-red
grapefruit (from 5 to 8 total)

**FOR ASSEMBLY**

1¼ cups heavy cream

¾ teaspoon
vanilla extract

¼ teaspoon orange-
blossom water (optional)

Cranberry Curd (page 233)

½ cup husked cape
gooseberries (optional)

**1.** Preheat oven to 250°F. Trace a 9-inch circle on a piece of parchment. Transfer parchment, traced-side down, to a baking sheet.

**2. Make the pavlova:** In a small bowl, stir together sugar and cornstarch. With an electric mixer, whisk egg whites with lemon juice and salt on low speed until frothy. Increase speed to medium-high and gradually add sugar mixture, beating until stiff, glossy peaks form, 10 to 12 minutes. Adhere corners of parchment to baking sheet with tiny dollops of meringue, then mound remaining meringue in center of circle on parchment. Using a large spoon, spread to edges of circle, leaving a well approximately 5 inches wide and 1 inch deep in center.

**3.** Bake until crisp and dry on outside but not developing any color, 1 hour 10 minutes to 1 hour 20 minutes. Turn oven off (do not open door); let cool in oven until dry and crisp on outside, at least 2 hours and up to 1 day.

**4. Suprême citrus:** Using a sharp knife and a cutting board, trim both ends of fruit. Set fruit on a trimmed end. Beginning at top and following curves of fruit, remove peel and pith. Working over a medium bowl to catch juice, carefully cut between membranes to release segments. Squeeze remaining membrane to extract juice, reserving for another use; discard membrane.

**5. To assemble:** In a medium bowl, whisk cream, vanilla, and orange-blossom water, if using, to soft peaks. Fill well of meringue with cranberry curd. Dollop cream over curd, top with citrus suprêmes and gooseberries, if desired, and serve immediately.

**BAKING TIP**

Don't peek! A pavlova requires low, slow heat and gradual cooling to bake and then dry out properly. Resist the temptation to open the oven door and let out the heat too quickly.

# Chocolate-and-Vanilla Zebra Cake

MAKES ONE 9-INCH LAYER CAKE

*A wild streak runs through this dessert beneath a coating of rich chocolate frosting. Cut a slice and reveal zebra-like stripes of vanilla and chocolate cake. It's a surprisingly easy trick to pull off—simply alternate spoonfuls of batter in the center of the pan to create concentric rings.*

### FOR THE CAKE

1 stick (½ cup) unsalted butter, melted, plus more for pans

4 cups unbleached all-purpose flour

1 tablespoon plus 1 teaspoon baking powder

2 teaspoons kosher salt

3 large eggs, separated, plus 4 more egg whites, room temperature

2½ cups granulated sugar

2 cups whole milk

½ cup safflower oil

1 tablespoon vanilla extract

½ cup unsweetened Dutch-process cocoa powder

### FOR THE FROSTING

⅔ cup unsweetened Dutch-process cocoa powder

1½ teaspoons instant espresso powder

½ teaspoon kosher salt

1 teaspoon vanilla extract

2½ sticks (1¼ cups) unsalted butter, room temperature

1½ cups confectioners' sugar

10 ounces semisweet chocolate, melted and cooled

3 tablespoons light corn syrup

**1. Make the cake:** Preheat oven to 350°F. Butter two 9-inch round cake pans. Line with parchment; butter parchment. In a large bowl, whisk together flour, baking powder, and salt until combined.

**2.** In a separate large bowl, whisk together all egg whites and granulated sugar until foamy, about 2 minutes. Whisk in 1½ cups milk, the butter, oil, and vanilla until smooth. Add flour mixture; whisk until smooth. In another large bowl, whisk together egg yolks, ⅓ cup milk, and the cocoa. Add 3¼ cups of vanilla batter to cocoa mixture and whisk until smooth. Whisk remaining milk into remaining vanilla batter.

**3.** Spoon ¼ cup vanilla batter into center of each prepared pan. Spoon ¼ cup chocolate batter into each center, directly on top of vanilla batter. Repeat, always spooning batter into center of pan and occasionally tapping pan firmly on counter, until all batter is used (batters should appear as concentric rings).

**4.** Bake, rotating pans halfway through, until cakes are puffed slightly and a cake tester comes out clean, 35 to 40 minutes. Transfer pans to a wire rack to cool 10 minutes. Turn out cakes onto rack to cool completely.

**5. Make the frosting:** Whisk together cocoa, espresso powder, salt, ½ cup hot water, and the vanilla until a smooth paste forms. In a large bowl with an electric mixer on medium-high speed, beat butter with confectioners' sugar until light and fluffy. Beat in chocolate and then cocoa mixture and corn syrup until smooth.

**6.** With a serrated knife, trim tops of cakes to level. Transfer a cake layer, trimmed-side up, to a cake plate or stand lined with parchment strips. Spread ¾ cup frosting evenly over top. Place remaining cake layer on top, trimmed-side down. Spread a thin layer of frosting over cake to form a crumb coat; refrigerate until firm, about 30 minutes. Spread remaining frosting evenly over top and sides of cake. Remove parchment strips and serve.

# Lemon Mousse Cake

MAKES ONE 9-INCH LAYER CAKE

*Lemon and meringue make one of the all-time great culinary duos. Here, they're whipped up into a light-as-air cake. A Swiss meringue frosting is piped on, and then toasted for a golden hue and to highlight its sensuous curves. A big pile of raspberries (we went for the gold) on top looks as if it's keeping the whole creation from floating away.*

## FOR THE CAKE

2 sticks (1 cup) unsalted butter, room temperature, cut into tablespoons, plus more for pans

3 cups cake flour (not self-rising), plus more for pans

1¼ cups whole milk

4 large eggs, room temperature

1 vanilla bean, split and seeds scraped

1¾ cups sugar

1 tablespoon baking powder

1 teaspoon kosher salt

Finely grated zest of 1 lemon

2 cups golden raspberries, for serving

**1. Make the cake:** Preheat oven to 350°F. Butter two 9-inch round cake pans. Line with parchment; butter parchment. Dust with flour, tapping out any excess. In a small bowl, whisk together milk, eggs, and vanilla seeds.

**2.** In a large bowl, with an electric mixer, beat together flour, sugar, baking powder, and salt on low speed until well combined. Continue beating while gradually adding butter until mixture is crumbly, about 3 minutes.

**3.** Slowly add half the milk mixture; increase speed to medium and beat until fluffy, about 2 minutes. Slowly add remaining half of milk mixture, scraping down sides of bowl as needed. Add lemon zest and beat until incorporated, about 1 minute more.

**4.** Divide batter evenly between prepared pans, smoothing tops with a small offset spatula. Bake until golden brown and a cake tester comes out clean, 35 to 40 minutes. Transfer pans to a wire rack; let cool completely. Turn cakes out of pans and remove parchment.

**5. Make the filling:** In a small bowl, sprinkle gelatin over cold water. Let stand until softened, about 5 minutes. In a small, heavy saucepan, whisk together yolks, sugar, and lemon zest and juice. Cook, whisking constantly, over medium-low heat, until mixture is thick enough to coat the back of a spoon, 8 to 10 minutes. Remove pan from heat; add gelatin mixture, stirring constantly, until gelatin is dissolved and mixture is slightly cool. Add butter, a few pieces at a time, stirring well after each addition, until smooth. Press filling through a fine sieve into a bowl. Cover with plastic wrap, pressing it directly onto surface to prevent skin from forming, and refrigerate until set, at least 2 hours and up to overnight. Stir filling; gently fold in whipped cream. Refrigerate 1 hour. Stir before using.

*(continued on page 49)*

**BAKING TIP**

A bit of acid helps
to stabilize Swiss
meringue; we use
vinegar here, but
lemon juice or cream
of tartar also work.
When whipping egg
whites for meringue,
be sure the beaters
and bowl are
thoroughly clean;
even the slightest
hint of oil or fat
can inhibit the foam.

## FOR THE FILLING

1½ teaspoons unflavored gelatin (from a ¼-ounce package)

½ cup cold water

6 large egg yolks

1 cup sugar

1 tablespoon plus 2 teaspoons finely grated lemon zest plus ¾ cup fresh juice (from 5 to 6 lemons)

1 stick (½ cup) cold unsalted butter, cut into small pieces

1 cup heavy cream, whipped to stiff peaks

## FOR THE SWISS MERINGUE

3 cups sugar

12 large egg whites, room temperature

Pinch of kosher salt

1 teaspoon vanilla extract

1 teaspoon cornstarch

1 teaspoon distilled white vinegar

**6.** With a serrated knife, trim tops of cakes to level; split each cake in half horizontally to form a total of 4 layers. Place a cake layer, bottom-side down, on a cake stand. Spread 1 heaping cup of filling to the edges with an offset spatula. Repeat process with 2 more cake layers. Top with remaining cake layer, bottom-side up. Refrigerate while you make meringue.

**7. Make the Swiss meringue:** In a heatproof bowl set over (not in) a pot of simmering water, combine sugar, egg whites, and salt. Whisk until sugar is dissolved and mixture is warm to the touch and feels completely smooth when rubbed between fingertips, 2 to 3 minutes. Remove bowl from heat. With an electric mixer, whisk on low speed until foamy. Increase speed to medium-high and whisk until stiff, glossy peaks form and mixture cools completely, about 10 minutes. Add vanilla, cornstarch, and vinegar; whisk until incorporated, about 1 minute more.

**8.** Evenly spread top and sides of cake with a ½-inch thickness of meringue, smoothing with an offset spatula. Transfer remaining meringue to a pastry bag fitted with a ¾-inch round tip. Position tip parallel to top of cake, about 1 inch from edge. Pipe meringue, using an even amount of pressure and dragging tip along surface and down side of cake, on the diagonal, and working from right to left. Continue piping, rotating cake, to cover completely. Use a kitchen torch to toast meringue, moving flame back and forth until evenly browned. Top with raspberries just before serving.

# Berry Layer Cake

**MAKES ONE 10-INCH LAYER CAKE**

*There's something fantastical about this triple-decker, berry-packed beauty. Whole fresh blueberries punctuate the dough, and black raspberry jam is blended into three batches of Swiss meringue buttercream, which is then piped into dreamlike rosettes and swirls. Too beautiful to eat? Maybe, but too delicious not to.*

---

2 sticks (1 cup) unsalted butter, cut into tablespoons, room temperature, plus more for pan

3 cups cake flour (not self-rising), plus more for pan

1¼ cups whole milk

4 large eggs, room temperature

1 vanilla bean, split and scraped

15 ounces fresh blueberries (about 2½ cups)

1 teaspoon cornstarch

1¾ cups sugar

1 tablespoon baking powder

1 teaspoon kosher salt

3 recipes Swiss Meringue Buttercream (page 237)

1½ cups seedless black raspberry jam

Gel-paste food coloring in burgundy

Fresh berries, such as blueberries, black raspberries, and blackberries, for garnish

**1.** Preheat oven to 350°F. Butter three 10-inch round cake pans. Line with parchment; butter parchment. Dust with flour, tapping out any excess. In a medium bowl, whisk together milk, eggs, and vanilla seeds. In a small bowl, toss blueberries with cornstarch. In a large bowl, with an electric mixer, beat flour, sugar, baking powder, and salt on low until well combined. Continue beating, gradually adding butter, until mixture is crumbly, about 3 minutes. Slowly add half the milk mixture; increase speed to medium and beat until fluffy, about 2 minutes. Gradually add remaining milk mixture, scraping down sides of bowl as needed. Beat until incorporated, about 1 minute more. Fold in blueberries.

**2.** Divide batter evenly among prepared pans, smoothing tops with an offset spatula. Bake, rotating pans halfway through, until tops are lightly golden and a cake tester comes out clean, about 30 minutes. Transfer pans to a wire rack to cool completely; turn out cakes.

**3.** Transfer all three batches of buttercream to a large bowl, reserving 2 cups. Fold jam into large bowl of buttercream. Add gel, one drop at a time, until desired shade is reached. With a serrated knife, trim tops of cake layers to level. Place a layer, bottom-side down, on a cake stand or platter, and spread with about 1½ cups berry buttercream. Top with second layer, bottom-side down, and 1½ cups berry buttercream. Top with third cake layer, bottom-side up. Spread a thin layer of frosting over cake to form a crumb coat; refrigerate until firm, about 30 minutes. Spread top and sides of cake evenly with a ½-inch thickness of berry buttercream, smoothing sides with an offset spatula.

**4.** Divide remaining berry buttercream among 3 bowls, and lighten each with some of reserved 2 cups white buttercream, creating different shades. Transfer to pastry bags fitted with open and closed star tips in a variety of sizes, such as #16, #22, #30, #35. Pipe swirls and rosettes of buttercream on top of cake. Serve cake garnished with berries as desired.

# Coffee Feather Cake

**MAKES ONE 8-INCH LAYER CAKE**

*Tiers of light, coffee-infused cake are layered with both dreamy mascarpone filling and coffee whipped cream, then adorned with shards of white, milk, and dark chocolates. To make the feathers, pour a spoonful of chocolate onto parchment and brush it into shape using a pastry brush—no piping required.*

### FOR THE CAKE

2¼ cups cake flour
(not self–rising)

1½ cups granulated sugar

1 tablespoon baking powder

1 teaspoon kosher salt

¾ cup strongly brewed coffee,
room temperature

½ cup safflower oil

6 large eggs, separated,
room temperature

1 tablespoon vanilla extract

### FOR THE MASCARPONE FILLING

1 cup mascarpone

Pinch of kosher salt

½ cup heavy cream

¼ cup confectioners' sugar

### FOR THE CHOCOLATE FEATHERS

1 ounce dark chocolate,
chopped (¼ cup)

1 ounce milk chocolate,
chopped (¼ cup)

2 ounces white chocolate,
chopped (½ cup)

### FOR THE COFFEE WHIPPED CREAM

½ cup granulated sugar

Pinch of kosher salt

1½ cups heavy cream

¼ cup strongly brewed
coffee, plus more to taste,
room temperature

**1. Make the cake:** Preheat oven to 325°F. In a large bowl, whisk together flour, ¾ cup granulated sugar, the baking powder, and salt. Add coffee, oil, egg yolks, and vanilla, and whisk until smooth.

**2.** With an electric mixer, whisk egg whites on medium speed until frothy, about 2 minutes. Increase speed to medium-high and gradually add remaining ¾ cup granulated sugar; beat until stiff, glossy peaks form, about 5 minutes. Gently fold egg whites into batter in two additions.

**3.** Divide batter evenly among three 8-inch round pans, smoothing tops with an offset spatula. Bake until lightly golden and tops spring back when pressed, 25 to 30 minutes. Transfer pans to a wire rack to cool 15 minutes. Run a small offset spatula around edges of cake pans and turn out cakes to cool completely, upside down. With a serrated knife, split each cake in half horizontally to form a total of 6 layers.

*(continued on page 55)*

**4. Make the mascarpone filling:** With an electric mixer, whisk mascarpone and salt on low speed until combined. With mixer running, slowly add heavy cream. Increase speed to medium and gradually add confectioners' sugar; beat to medium peaks. Store, covered, in refrigerator until ready to use.

**5. Make the chocolate feathers:** Melt each chocolate in a separate heatproof bowl set over (not in) a pan of simmering water, stirring until smooth. Mix a little milk chocolate into half of the melted white chocolate to create a fourth color. Working in batches, spoon half-dollar-size pools of melted chocolate onto baking sheets lined with nonstick baking mats or parchment. Using pastry brushes and short, quick strokes, brush melted chocolate into feather shapes. Refrigerate feathers for at least 30 minutes to set.

**6. Make the coffee whipped cream:** With an electric mixer, whisk granulated sugar, salt, heavy cream, and coffee on medium-low to dissolve sugar, about 1 minute. Increase speed to medium-high and whip to stiff peaks, about 3 minutes. For a stronger coffee flavor, whisk in an additional 1 to 2 tablespoons coffee.

**7.** Anchor a cake layer, bottom-side down, on an 8-inch board with a dab of whipped cream. Spread ¾ cup mascarpone filling evenly over cake layer, then top with a second cake layer. Spread evenly with ¾ cup coffee whipped cream, then repeat the process, alternating mascarpone filling and coffee whipped cream between layers, ending with sixth and final cake layer, bottom-side up. Spread a thin layer of coffee whipped cream over cake to form a crumb coat; refrigerate until firm, about 15 minutes. Spread remaining coffee whipped cream over top and sides of cake. Create a layering effect with chocolate feathers by attaching them, on a slight angle, to side of cake with a dab of whipped cream to anchor them.

**DECORATING TIP**

To create the feather adornments, spoon pools of melted chocolate on a parchment-lined sheet. Using a 1½-inch pastry brush and short, quick strokes, brush the melted chocolate into feather shapes of varying lengths; then chill until set.

# Raspberry and Chocolate-Hazelnut Crepe Cake

### SERVES 10 TO 12

*This impressive no-bake dessert is built on a tall stack of crepes—which can be made ahead of time—layered with both white chocolate-raspberry and dark chocolate-hazelnut whipped cream fillings. The assembled cake will need to chill for at least eight hours (and up to two days) in order to set and slice neatly, so plan to make it the day before serving.*

---

**FOR THE CREPES**

2 cups unbleached all-purpose flour

2 tablespoons granulated sugar

½ teaspoon kosher salt

3 cups whole milk

8 large eggs

6 tablespoons unsalted butter, melted, plus more for skillet

**FOR THE FILLINGS**

2¼ teaspoons unflavored gelatin (1 envelope)

⅓ cup cold water

1 cup seedless raspberry jam (12 ounces)

3 ounces white chocolate, melted

1 cup chocolate-hazelnut spread, such as Nutella

3 ounces bittersweet chocolate (61 to 70% cacao), melted

3 cups heavy cream

⅓ cup confectioners' sugar, sifted, plus more for serving

Fresh raspberries, for serving

**1. Make the crepes:** In a blender, purée flour, granulated sugar, salt, milk, eggs, and butter until smooth, about 30 seconds. Refrigerate at least 30 minutes and up to 1 day; stir before using.

**2.** Heat an 8-inch nonstick skillet over medium; lightly brush with butter. Add a scant ¼ cup batter, tilting and swirling skillet until it evenly coats bottom. Cook until crepe is golden in places and edges lift from pan, 1 to 1½ minutes. Flip and cook until just set, about 45 seconds. Slide crepe onto a paper towel–lined plate. Repeat with remaining batter, coating pan with more butter as needed and stacking crepes directly on top of one another (you should finish with about 30). Let cool completely. (Crepes can be covered and refrigerated up to 1 day.)

**3. Make the fillings:** In a small bowl, sprinkle gelatin over cold water. Let stand until softened, about 5 minutes. Meanwhile, heat jam in a small saucepan over medium heat until hot. Remove from heat; stir in gelatin mixture until dissolved (mixture should feel smooth when rubbed between your fingers). Transfer to a large bowl and whisk in white chocolate until smooth. In another bowl, stir together hazelnut spread and bittersweet chocolate until smooth. In a clean bowl, whisk cream and confectioners' sugar to stiff peaks. Divide whipped cream evenly between raspberry and hazelnut mixtures (about 3 cups each), and stir until smooth. Refrigerate cream mixtures until thickened slightly but still spreadable, at least 1 hour and up to 2 hours.

**4.** To make cake, place a crepe on a cake plate. Spread ⅓ cup raspberry-cream mixture evenly over crepe, leaving a ¼-inch border. Top with another crepe; spread with ⅓ cup hazelnut-cream mixture. Repeat layering, alternating fillings, until all crepes are used, finishing with a crepe. Loosely cover with plastic wrap and refrigerate until cold and set, at least 8 hours and up to 2 days. Just before serving, top cake with raspberries and dust generously with confectioners' sugar.

**SERVING TIP**

For the cleanest slices, chill the crepe cake before serving and cut it with a very sharp knife.

# Eggnog Semifreddo Genoise

## SERVES 10 TO 12

*This knockout cake is for the confident baker, as it takes time and careful technique. But the effort will be worth it for the raves you'll get after serving up the first slice. To make the dramatically striped interior, nutmeg-and-rum-scented semifreddo is spread onto dark chocolate genoise, which is then rolled and layered on its side.*

---

### FOR THE CAKE

Vegetable cooking spray

½ cup sifted unsweetened Dutch-process cocoa powder, plus more for dusting

1 cup sifted cake flour (not self-rising)

½ teaspoon kosher salt

6 large eggs plus 4 large egg yolks, room temperature

1 cup sugar

1 stick (½ cup) unsalted butter, melted and cooled

### FOR THE FILLING

2¼ teaspoons unflavored gelatin (1 envelope)

⅓ cup light rum

4 large eggs, separated, room temperature

1¼ cups sugar

2½ cups cold heavy cream

½ teaspoon freshly grated nutmeg

2 teaspoons vanilla extract

Swiss Meringue Frosting (page 237)

**1. Make the cake:** Preheat oven to 425°F. Coat two 12½-by-17½-inch rimmed baking sheets with cooking spray. Line with parchment; spray parchment. Dust with cocoa, tapping out any excess. Dust 2 clean kitchen towels with cocoa. In a medium bowl, whisk together cocoa, flour, and salt.

**2.** In a heatproof bowl set over (not in) a pot of simmering water, combine eggs, yolks, and sugar. Whisk until sugar is dissolved and mixture is warm to the touch, about 2 minutes. With an electric mixer on medium-high speed, beat about 2 minutes. Increase speed to high and beat until mixture is pale and thick, about 3 minutes more.

**3.** Pour melted butter down side of bowl; gently fold to combine, scraping bottom of bowl to make sure dry ingredients are fully incorporated. Divide batter evenly between prepared sheets, smoothing tops with an offset spatula. Bake until center springs back when lightly touched, 5 to 7 minutes. Remove sheets and turn out cakes onto prepared towels. Immediately, starting at one short side, roll a cake into a log, incorporating the towel. Repeat with second cake. Let cool while preparing filling.

*(continued on page 61)*

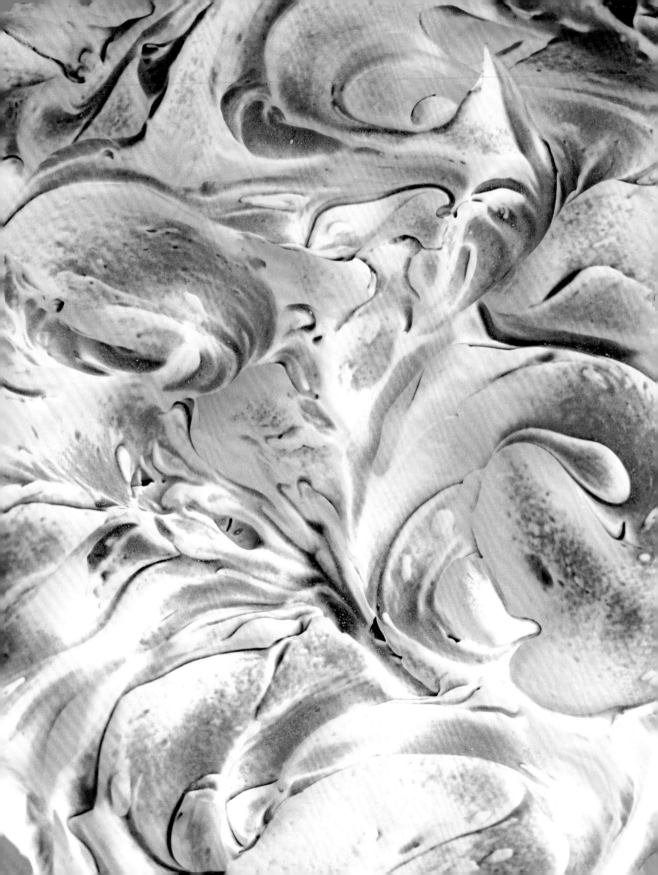

**4. Make the filling:** In a small bowl, sprinkle gelatin over rum; let stand until softened, about 5 minutes. In a heatproof bowl set over (not in) a pot of simmering water, combine egg yolks and ¾ cup sugar. Whisk until pale and fluffy, about 2 minutes. Remove from heat; whisk in gelatin mixture. Set bowl over pot of simmering water again and whisk until gelatin is dissolved. Transfer mixture to a medium bowl.

**5.** In a medium mixing bowl with an electric mixer on medium-high speed, whisk cream with nutmeg and vanilla to medium peaks (the tips of the peaks curl over when the beaters are lifted). Fold one-third of whipped cream into gelatin mixture, then fold gelatin mixture into remaining whipped cream. In a clean mixing bowl, whisk egg whites and remaining ½ cup sugar on medium-high speed to stiff peaks, about 6 minutes. Fold into cream mixture.

**6.** Unroll cooled cakes, remove towels, and transfer each to a separate rimmed baking sheet. Set aside 1 cup filling; spread remaining filling between cakes. Freeze cakes until filling starts to firm up but is still pliable, about 20 minutes.

**7.** With a serrated knife, slice each cake in half lengthwise to create a total of 4 cake strips. Starting at a short end of one strip, roll up cake and place it vertically in the center of a cake stand. Starting where rolled strip ends, wrap next strip around cake. Continue to wrap with remaining strips. Use reserved filling to fill in top of cake. For added stability, wrap a parchment collar around base of cake, keeping bottom of paper flush with cake stand. Freeze until firm, at least 8 hours and up to 2 days. Once frozen, trim top of cake with a serrated knife to level. Keep frozen until ready to frost.

**8.** Spread frosting evenly over top and sides of cake with an offset spatula, using an S motion to create a textured appearance. Freeze cake at least 30 minutes and up to 1 day. Use a kitchen torch to toast meringue, moving flame back and forth until evenly browned; serve immediately.

**BAKING TIP**

The key to a light genoise is air—the more air you incorporate when whipping the eggs, the lighter the cake will be. Beat them on high speed until they are pale white, doubled in volume, and hold a thick ribbon.

# Grasshopper Ice-Cream Cake

## SERVES 12

*Bake this gorgeous cake in a bowl to give it a dome shape; then coat
its hollowed-out insides with a layer of chocolate to seal the cake before packing
it with ice cream. We love the mint and chocolate of a classic
grasshopper, but you could adapt this with your favorite flavor combinations.*

---

### FOR THE CAKE

½ cup safflower oil,
plus more for bowl

1½ cups unsweetened
Dutch-process cocoa powder,
plus more for bowl

3 cups unbleached
all-purpose flour

3 cups sugar

1 tablespoon baking soda

1½ teaspoons baking powder

1½ teaspoons kosher salt

4 large eggs, room temperature

1½ cups buttermilk

1½ cups warm water

2 teaspoons vanilla extract

4 ounces semisweet
chocolate, melted and
cooled slightly

6 cups mint–chocolate–chip
ice cream, softened

### FOR THE GLAZE

9 ounces semisweet
chocolate, chopped (about
1⅔ cups)

1 stick (½ cup) unsalted
butter, cut into tablespoons,
room temperature

3 tablespoons light corn syrup

**1. Make the cake:** Preheat oven to 350°F. Brush bottom and sides of a large (approximately 10 inches in diameter and 5 inches deep) ovenproof glass or metal bowl with oil. Dust with cocoa, tapping out any excess.

**2.** In a large bowl, whisk together cocoa, flour, sugar, baking soda, baking powder, and salt until thoroughly combined. Add oil, eggs, buttermilk, warm water, and vanilla; whisk until smooth, about 2 minutes. Transfer to prepared bowl.

**3.** Bake until set and a cake tester comes out clean, 1 hour 25 minutes to 1 hour 45 minutes. Transfer bowl to a wire rack to cool 15 minutes. Turn out cake onto rack to cool completely.

**4.** With a serrated knife, cut a 1-inch-thick slice from bottom of cake and set aside. Invert cake "bowl"; using a metal spoon, hollow out all but a 1-inch border of cake (reserve scraps for snacking!). Brush hollowed-out cake bowl and cut side of cake bottom with melted chocolate. Refrigerate until chocolate is firm, about 20 minutes.

**5.** Spoon softened ice cream into cake bowl, smoothing top with an offset spatula. Return bottom of cake to bowl (it will be on top at this point). Cover with plastic; freeze until ice cream is firm, at least 4 hours and up to 3 days.

**6. Make the glaze:** Unwrap cake and place it, dome-side up, on a rimmed baking sheet lined with a wire rack. In a heatproof bowl set over (not in) a saucepan of simmering water, place chocolate, butter, and corn syrup. Stir occasionally until melted and smooth, and immediately pour over top center of cake all at once. (Gently shake baking sheet and tap it on counter so that glaze covers cake.) Using two large, wide spatulas, transfer to a serving plate. Serve immediately or freeze, uncovered, up to 1 day; remove from freezer 10 to 15 minutes before serving. To serve, use a knife dipped in hot water and then wiped dry to cut into wedges.

**BAKING TIP**

The whole cake
bakes in one pan—
rising up tall—and is
sliced horizontally
into layers once
cool. If you don't
have a springform
pan, an 8-inch
round cake pan will
do just as well.

# Vanilla Sponge Cake with Strawberry Meringue

*Let us present the modern-day strawberry shortcake: Tall, light, and oh-so-gorgeous, this ethereal sponge cake calls for three pounds of plump, ripe strawberries—sandwiched between the cake layers as well as piled high on top—to ensure each bite includes the rosy fruit. Strawberry fields forever, indeed.*

## FOR THE CAKE

Vegetable cooking spray

2¼ cups cake flour (not self–rising)

1½ cups granulated sugar

2¼ teaspoons baking powder

¾ teaspoon kosher salt

1 stick (½ cup) unsalted butter, melted and cooled slightly

7 large eggs, separated, room temperature

⅔ cup whole milk, room temperature

½ teaspoon cream of tartar

2 teaspoons vanilla extract

Confectioners' sugar, for dusting (optional)

## FOR THE FROSTING

3 pounds strawberries, hulled

1¾ cups granulated sugar

7 large egg whites, room temperature

¼ teaspoon kosher salt

4 sticks (2 cups) unsalted butter, cut into pieces, room temperature

1 teaspoon vanilla extract

**1. Make the cake:** Preheat oven to 325°F. Coat an 8-inch springform pan with cooking spray. Line sides with a 5-inch-wide strip of parchment and spray parchment.

**2.** In a medium bowl, whisk together flour, ¾ cup granulated sugar, the baking powder, and salt until thoroughly combined. In a large bowl, whisk together butter, egg yolks, and milk to combine. Whisk flour mixture into butter mixture until smooth.

**3.** With an electric mixer, beat egg whites on medium-low speed until frothy, about 2 minutes. Add cream of tartar and vanilla, and beat on medium-high speed until soft peaks form, about 2 minutes more. Gradually add remaining ¾ cup granulated sugar and beat until stiff, glossy peaks form, about 5 minutes. Whisk one-third of egg-white mixture into batter. Gently but thoroughly fold in remaining egg-white mixture with a rubber spatula. Transfer batter to prepared pan, smoothing top with an offset spatula.

**4.** Bake until risen and golden brown and a cake tester comes out clean, about 45 minutes. Reduce oven to 300°F and continue to bake until top springs back when lightly touched, about 35 minutes more. Transfer pan to a wire rack to cool 10 minutes. Unlock pan and carefully lift to remove. Remove parchment and turn cake out onto rack, running a sharp knife between cake and pan bottom to release. Remove bottom and turn cake top-side up; let cool completely.

*(continued on page 67)*

**5. Make the frosting:** In a food processor, purée 1 pound strawberries with ½ cup granulated sugar until smooth. Transfer to a medium saucepan and bring to a boil. Reduce heat to medium and cook, stirring frequently, until darkened, thick, and syrupy, about 10 minutes. Strain through a fine-mesh sieve, pressing on solids to remove as much liquid as possible (you should have about 1 cup). Refrigerate, covered, until cooled to room temperature, about 1 hour (or transfer to a bowl set in an ice-water bath and stir occasionally until cool to the touch, about 10 minutes).

**6.** In a heatproof bowl set over (not in) a pot of simmering water, combine egg whites, remaining 1¼ cups granulated sugar, and the salt, whisking constantly until sugar is dissolved and mixture is warm, about 2 minutes. (It should feel completely smooth when rubbed between your fingertips.) Remove bowl from heat. With an electric mixer, starting on low speed and gradually increasing to medium-high, beat egg whites until stiff, glossy peaks form. Continue beating until bottom of bowl is cool to the touch, about 10 minutes.

**7.** Reduce speed to medium-low and beat in butter, a few tablespoons at a time, until combined, scraping down sides of bowl as needed. Slowly add strawberry purée and vanilla, beating until combined. (If buttercream appears curdled, increase speed to medium-high and beat until smooth.)

**8.** Slice 1 pound strawberries lengthwise, ¼ inch thick (you should have about 2½ cups). With a serrated knife, trim top of cake to level; split cake horizontally into 3 even layers. Transfer bottom layer, cut-side up, to a cake stand lined with parchment strips. Spread evenly with ¾ cup buttercream and top with half of sliced strawberries. Spread another ¾ cup buttercream onto middle cake layer and place over first cake layer, frosted-side down. Press gently to adhere, being careful not to allow strawberries to slide out. Spread top with another ¾ cup buttercream; top evenly with remaining sliced strawberries. Spread another ¾ cup buttercream onto cut side of top cake layer; place on center cake, frosted-side down, pressing gently to adhere.

**9.** Using a small offset metal spatula, spread remaining buttercream evenly over top and sides of cake. Top cake with remaining 1 pound strawberries, cutting some in half, if desired. Dust lightly with confectioners' sugar, if using, and serve. (This cake is best assembled, kept at room temperature, and served the same day, but it can be refrigerated, uncovered, up to 1 day; bring to room temperature before serving.)

# Splatter Cake with Passionfruit Curd

## MAKES ONE 8-INCH LAYER CAKE

*Channel your inner Jackson Pollock with this modern-art-inspired layer cake. With a rich chocolate cake, passionfruit curd filling, and smooth meringue buttercream, it's as delicious as it is fun. Use small pastry brushes to create the splatter design, and luster dust in shades of pink and copper as your "paint."*

Safflower oil, for pan

²/₃ cup strong, hot coffee

½ cup unsweetened Dutch-process cocoa powder

1¾ cups cake flour (not self-rising)

1½ cups sugar

2¼ teaspoons baking powder

¾ teaspoon kosher salt

1 stick (½ cup) unsalted butter, melted and cooled

7 large eggs, separated, room temperature,

½ teaspoon cream of tartar

2 teaspoons vanilla extract

Swiss Meringue Buttercream (page 237)

Passionfruit Curd (page 232)

Luster dust in dark pink, light pink, and copper

Vodka or grain alcohol

**SPECIAL EQUIPMENT**

2 small pastry brushes, for splattering

**1.** Preheat oven to 325°F. Lightly coat three 8-inch round cake pans with safflower oil. Line with parchment; lightly oil parchment. In a small bowl, whisk together coffee and cocoa until smooth; let cool, about 10 minutes. In a medium bowl, whisk together flour, ¾ cup sugar, the baking powder, and salt.

**2.** In a large bowl, whisk together butter, egg yolks, and coffee mixture. Whisk in flour mixture until smooth. With an electric mixer, whisk egg whites on medium-low speed until frothy, 1 to 2 minutes. Add cream of tartar and vanilla. Increase speed to medium-high and beat until soft peaks form, about 2 minutes more. Gradually add remaining ¾ cup sugar and beat until stiff, glossy peaks form, 5 to 7 minutes. Whisk one-third of egg-white mixture into batter until smooth, then fold in remainder.

**3.** Divide batter evenly among prepared pans, smoothing tops with an offset spatula. Bake until tops spring back when lightly pressed with a finger, 20 to 25 minutes. Transfer pans to a wire rack to cool 10 minutes. Turn out cakes onto rack to cool completely.

**4.** With a serrated knife, trim tops of cakes to level. Using a dab of buttercream, anchor a layer on top of a cake board. Transfer 1 cup buttercream to a pastry bag and snip off the end. Pipe a ring around perimeter and fill with ½ cup passionfruit curd. (The dam will hold the filling in place.) Top with a second cake layer and repeat process, then finish with final cake layer, bottom-side up. Transfer cake to refrigerator to allow to set, at least 30 minutes. Spread a thin layer of buttercream over cake to form a crumb coat; refrigerate until firm, about 15 minutes. Frost cake with remaining buttercream and chill again, at least 30 minutes.

**5.** In 3 small bowls, mix ¼ teaspoon of each luster dust with a small amount of vodka, 1 tablespoon at a time, until a thin but not watery paint mixture forms (the consistency should be that of whole milk). Using brushes, splatter paints all over cake until desired look is achieved.

**DECORATING TIP**

For long lines, hold a brush at
the end of the handle and
snap your wrist as you splatter
luster dust onto the cake.
For short sprays, hold the brush
about 2 inches from
the cake surface and rub your
thumb over the bristles.

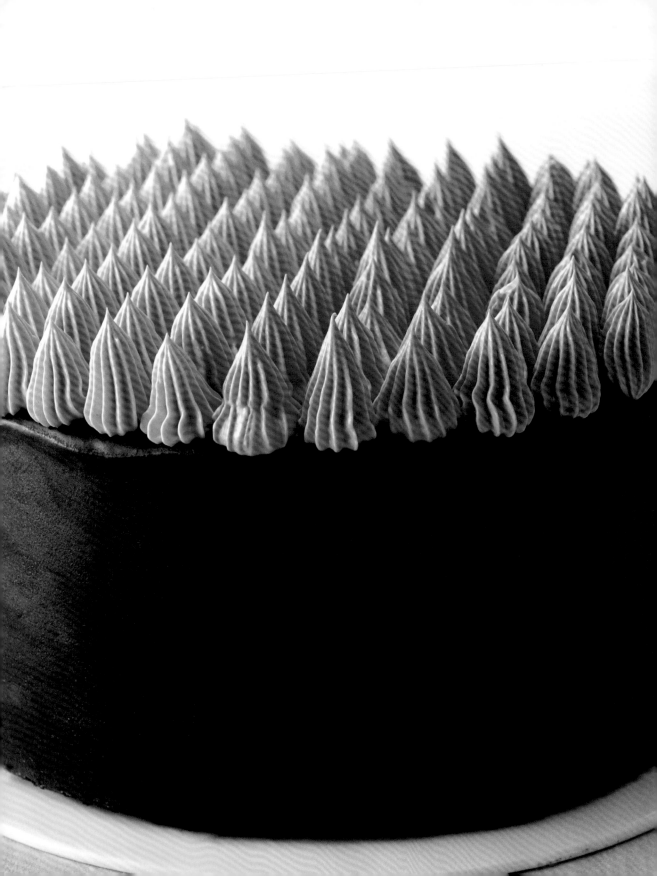

# Starburst Cake

## MAKES ONE 9-INCH LAYER CAKE

*Master a single piping technique—the icing starburst—and you can re-create
this cheerful cake. The layers are first coated with a pourable ganache,
allowed to set, and then piped with rows of icing stars in a subtle range of hues.
The first step? Baking the cake of your choice—white, lemon, or chocolate.*

Two 9-inch-cakes
(see Mix-and-Match Cakes,
page 226)

Whipped Ganache
Frosting (page 241)

Chocolate Ganache
Glaze (page 241)

Swiss Meringue
Buttercream (page 237)

Gel-paste food coloring
in lemon yellow,
warm brown, and soft pink

**1.** With a serrated knife, trim tops of cake layers to level. Place a layer, bottom-side down, on a wire rack set over a parchment-lined rimmed baking sheet. Spread ¼ cup frosting evenly over cake layer. Place second layer, cut-side down, on top. Spread a thin layer of whipped ganache frosting over cake to form a crumb coat; refrigerate until firm, about 30 minutes.

**2.** Slowly pour chocolate ganache glaze over top and down sides of cake (use an offset spatula to spread evenly, if needed). Refrigerate until set, about 15 minutes. Scrape excess glaze into a bowl, passing it through a fine-mesh sieve to remove any crumbs. Pour a second coat of glaze over cake; refrigerate until set, about 15 minutes.

**3.** Divide buttercream among 4 bowls; tint to desired shades with gel (we used the colors listed to mix 2 shades each of yellow and peach). Transfer buttercream to 4 pastry bags fitted with an open-star tip (such as Ateco #864 or Wilton #4B).

**4.** Mark a line across the center of cake's surface with a toothpick to serve as a guide. Holding bag at a 90-degree angle, gently squeeze; then release halfway into each peak, drawing tip up until buttercream forms a point. Pipe a line of stars across center, following the line, then add more rows, working from center out and changing colors every few rows to create an ombré effect.

# 2
# Layer Cakes

*Two cake layers is nice, three is better.*
*But why stop there when you can go a mile high (especially*
*if it's chocolate)? The rule of thumb*
*on baking these towering tiers: even layers, generous*
*fillings, and don't forget the crumb coat.*

———

# Meyer Lemon and Coconut Layer Cake

MAKES ONE 7-INCH LAYER CAKE

*With its candied lemon slices and fresh mint sprigs, this memorable cake will brighten anyone's day. Tucked between each luscious layer is a lemon-coconut curd that includes two types of lemons—Meyer, for their sweetness and aroma, and standard ones, for their beloved tartness.*

7 tablespoons unsalted butter, cut into pieces, room temperature, plus more for pans

3 cups unbleached all-purpose flour, plus more for pans

1 cup sweetened shredded coconut

1 cup whole milk, room temperature

4 large eggs, room temperature

1 teaspoon vanilla extract

1²⁄₃ cups sugar

1 tablespoon baking powder

1½ teaspoons kosher salt

¼ cup raw, unrefined coconut oil (2 ounces), room temperature (solid)

Coconut Lemon Curd (page 232)

Coconut Buttercream (page 239)

Candied Citrus Slices (page 244) and fresh mint leaves, for serving

**1.** Preheat oven to 350°F. Butter two 7-inch round cake pans. Line with parchment; butter parchment. Dust with flour, tapping out any excess. Spread coconut in an even layer on a baking sheet and bake until dry but not golden, about 10 minutes; let cool completely.

**2.** In a medium bowl, whisk milk into eggs, then whisk in vanilla. With an electric mixer, beat flour, sugar, baking powder, and salt on medium-low speed for 30 seconds. Continue beating while gradually adding butter and coconut oil until mixture is crumbly, about 3 minutes. Slowly add half of milk mixture; increase speed to medium and beat until fluffy, about 1 minute. Slowly add remaining milk mixture, scraping down sides of bowl as needed. Beat until incorporated, about 30 seconds.

**3.** Divide batter evenly between prepared pans, smoothing tops with an offset spatula; tap pans on counter. Bake until golden brown and tops spring back when lightly touched, 50 to 55 minutes. Transfer pans to a wire rack to cool 10 minutes. Turn out cakes onto rack to cool completely.

**4.** With a serrated knife, trim tops of cakes layers to level; split each in half horizontally to form a total of 4 layers. Place a cake layer, bottom-side down, on a cake plate. Spread ⅔ cup curd evenly over it; top with a second cake layer. Repeat, spreading ⅔ cup curd between each layer. Finish with a cake layer, bottom-side up. Refrigerate cake, wrapped in plastic, at least 1 hour and up to 1 day.

**5.** Spread 1 cup buttercream over top and sides of cake evenly to create a crumb coat. Refrigerate 15 minutes. Spread remaining 3 cups buttercream over top and sides. Coat sides with baked coconut. Garnish with candied lemon and mint and serve. (Cake can be refrigerated, wrapped in plastic, up to 5 days; return to room temperature before serving.)

**BAKING TIP**

After filling the pans
with batter, tap them
lightly on a counter to
force air bubbles
to the surface; this will
prevent holes from
forming in the cake.

**DECORATING TIP**

To achieve this design, we cut out a wave-like template and laid it atop the baked kremówka; then sifted confectioners' sugar over it. You can create a simple template to make a pattern or work freehand, using any design you like.

# Kremówka

SERVES 12

*Polish bakers call this dessert* kremówka *(pronounced kreh-MOOV-kah), meaning "cream cake," and that's exactly what it is. Like a big, fluffy Napoleon, a mousseline of vanilla pastry cream and creamed butter get sandwiched between golden-brown puff pastry. For graphic appeal, we sifted confectioners' sugar in waves along the top.*

1 pound puff pastry, preferably all butter (thawed, if frozen)

¾ cup granulated sugar, plus more for rolling

6 tablespoons cornstarch

Pinch of kosher salt

3 cups whole milk

6 large egg yolks

3 sticks (1½ cups) unsalted butter plus 3 tablespoons, room temperature

1 vanilla bean, split and seeds scraped

Confectioners' sugar, sifted, for dusting

**1.** Preheat oven to 400°F with racks in upper and lower thirds. Line 2 baking sheets with nonstick baking mats or parchment. Divide puff pastry into 2 equal pieces. Sprinkle work surface with granulated sugar and roll out each piece of pastry to a 9-by-13-inch rectangle. Transfer to prepared baking sheets, sugar-side up, and bake, rotating sheets halfway through, until puffed and deep golden brown, about 35 minutes. Transfer sheets to a wire rack to cool completely.

**2.** In a medium saucepan, whisk together granulated sugar, cornstarch, and salt. In a medium bowl, whisk together milk and egg yolks. Add milk mixture to saucepan, along with 3 tablespoons butter. Cook, stirring, over medium heat until mixture comes to a boil; let boil 1 minute. Strain pastry cream through a fine-mesh sieve into a medium bowl. Cover with plastic wrap, pressing it directly onto the surface. Refrigerate until chilled, at least 2 hours and up to 2 days.

**3.** With an electric mixer, beat remaining 3 sticks butter on medium speed until smooth. Reduce speed to low and add vanilla seeds and cooled pastry cream, ½ cup at a time. Increase speed to medium-high, and beat until light and fluffy, about 2 minutes.

**4.** Place a rectangle of puff pastry on a cutting board and spread with pastry cream mixture. Top with second puff pastry rectangle and press gently to adhere. Loosely cover and refrigerate until set, at least 1 hour and up to 8 hours. Dust confectioners' sugar on top in desired design. To serve, slice with a serrated knife into 3-inch squares.

# Devil's Food Cake

**MAKES ONE 9-INCH LAYER CAKE**

*Here's a devil's food that's extra devilish: Melted chocolate in addition to the usual cocoa powder gives it a deeper chocolate flavor, and sour cream helps it stay ultra moist. We finished this cake with a classic chocolate buttercream, but a Seven-Minute Frosting (page 238) would be just as irresistible if that's your weakness.*

---

3 sticks (1½ cups) unsalted butter, room temperature, plus more for pans

1 cup boiling water

¾ cup unsweetened Dutch-process cocoa powder

4 ounces bittersweet chocolate (61 to 70% cacao), chopped (¾ cup)

3½ cups unbleached all-purpose flour

1 teaspoon baking powder

¾ teaspoon baking soda

1½ teaspoons kosher salt

2 cups packed light-brown sugar

4 large eggs, room temperature

2 teaspoons vanilla extract

1 cup sour cream

6¼ cups Chocolate Swiss Meringue Buttercream (page 238)

**1.** Preheat oven to 325°F. Butter two 9-inch round cake pans. Line with parchment; butter parchment. In a medium bowl, stir together boiling water, cocoa, and chocolate; let cool 10 minutes. In another medium bowl, whisk together flour, baking powder, baking soda, and salt.

**2.** With an electric mixer on medium-high speed, beat butter with sugar until fluffy, 2 to 3 minutes. Add eggs, one at a time, beating well after each addition and scraping down sides of bowl as needed. Beat in vanilla, then chocolate mixture. Reduce speed to low; beat in flour mixture in two additions, alternating with sour cream, until just combined.

**3.** Divide batter evenly between prepared pans, smoothing tops with an offset spatula. Bake until a cake tester comes out with a few moist crumbs attached, 35 to 40 minutes. Transfer pans to a wire rack to cool 20 minutes. Turn out cakes onto rack to cool completely.

**4.** With a serrated knife, trim tops of cakes layers to level. Transfer one cake, trimmed-side up, to a cake plate or stand lined with parchment strips. Spread evenly with 1½ cups buttercream. Top with remaining cake layer, trimmed-side down. Spread a thin layer of buttercream over top and sides to create a crumb coat. Refrigerate until firm, about 30 minutes. Spread remaining frosting evenly over top and sides. (Cake can be stored in refrigerator up to 1 day; bring to room temperature before serving.)

**BAKING TIP**

While the cake layers cool, toast the walnuts in the oven at 350°F: Spread them in a single layer on a parchment-lined baking sheet, tossing occasionally, until golden and fragrant, 8 to 10 minutes.

# Milk-and-Cookies Cake

*This is what happens when your favorite childhood dessert grows up. We created this elegant cake with milk and cookies in mind: The batter is brown sugar–tinged, for a cookie-dough-like flavor, and flecked with miniature chocolate chips— plus toffee for a caramel crunch. And the milk? A luscious crème anglaise buttercream.*

---

### FOR THE CAKE

2 sticks (1 cup) unsalted butter, room temperature, plus more for pans

3 cups cake flour (not self-rising), plus more for pans

1 tablespoon baking powder

½ teaspoon kosher salt

1 cup packed dark–brown sugar

⅔ cup granulated sugar

4 large eggs plus 2 large egg yolks

1 tablespoon vanilla extract

1½ cups buttermilk

1½ cups mini chocolate chips, plus more for decorating

### FOR THE WALNUT TOFFEE CRUNCH

6 tablespoons unsalted butter

½ cup plus 2 tablespoons granulated sugar

1 cup walnut halves, toasted

½ teaspoon kosher salt

### FOR THE CRÈME ANGLAISE BUTTERCREAM

10 large egg whites

2¼ cups granulated sugar

8 sticks (4 cups) unsalted butter, room temperature

1 tablespoon vanilla extract

¼ cup nonfat dry milk powder

**1. Make the cake:** Preheat oven to 350°F. Brush two 9-inch round cake pans with butter. Line with parchment; butter parchment. Dust with flour, tapping out any excess.

**2.** In a large bowl, whisk together cake flour, baking powder, and salt. With an electric mixer, beat butter and both sugars on high speed until light and fluffy, about 6 minutes. Add whole eggs and egg yolks, one at a time, beating well after each addition until combined. Beat in vanilla extract. With mixer on low, add flour mixture to butter mixture in three batches, alternating with butter-milk, beginning and ending with flour, and scraping down sides of bowl as needed. Stir in mini chocolate chips.

**3.** Divide batter evenly between prepared pans, smoothing tops with an offset spatula. Bake until cake tester comes out clean, about 35 minutes. Transfer pans to a wire rack to cool 10 minutes. Turn out cakes onto rack to cool completely.

*(continued on page 83)*

**DECORATING TIP**

To create a Swiss dot pattern around the sides of the cake, apply a total of five rows of mini chocolate chips: Begin with a row in the center of the cake, applying each chocolate chip approximately 1½ inches apart. Repeat a row, 1½ inches above and below the initial one. Apply the final two rows in between the top and center rows, and then between the center and bottom rows. Offset the placement of the first chip by approximately ¾ inch, centering it between two chips in the above row.

**4. Make the walnut toffee crunch:** In a medium saucepan, heat butter and granulated sugar over high, stirring, until butter is melted. Continue to cook, stirring occasionally, until mixture is dark amber, 8 to 10 minutes more. Add toasted walnuts and salt, and stir to combine; transfer immediately to a baking sheet lined with a nonstick baking mat to set. Once cooled, roughly chop.

**5. Make the buttercream:** In bowl set over (not in) a saucepan of simmering water, whisk together egg whites and granulated sugar. Cook, whisking occasionally, until mixture is completely smooth when rubbed between two fingers, 3 to 5 minutes. Remove bowl from heat. With an electric mixer, whisk on low speed for 1 minute; then increase speed to medium-high and beat until stiff, glossy peaks form, 7 to 10 minutes. Reduce speed to medium-low and add butter, a few pieces at a time, until all is incorporated. Add vanilla, and then nonfat milk powder, and whisk to combine. Switch to the paddle attachment and beat on low speed about 2 minutes to remove any air bubbles.

**6. For assembly:** With a serrated knife, split each cake in half horizontally to form a total of 4 layers. Anchor bottom layer on a cake board with a dab of buttercream. Spread a generous 1 cup buttercream evenly over cake layer, then top with one-third of walnut toffee crunch. Top with second cake layer, pressing down lightly to adhere. Repeat process, finishing with final cake layer bottom-side up. Spread a thin, even layer of buttercream over top and sides to create a crumb coat. Refrigerate about 30 minutes. Spread remaining frosting evenly over top and sides, finishing top with a decorative swirl, if desired. Using remaining mini chocolate chips, create a Swiss dot pattern around sides of cake. Refrigerate until firm, about 30 minutes. Bring to room temperature before serving.

# Spumoni Cake

**SERVES 6 TO 8**

*This nostalgic ice cream cake is sure to charm kids and adults alike. That familiar trio of ice cream flavors—pistachio, vanilla, and strawberry—is layered with chewy cornbread cake and frosted with whipped cream for a take on spumoni. You can make it up to two weeks before serving; just keep it well wrapped in the freezer.*

1 stick (½ cup) unsalted butter, melted, plus more for brushing

¾ cup granulated sugar

Finely grated zest of 1 lemon

2 large eggs

½ teaspoon kosher salt

½ cup unbleached all-purpose flour

½ cup fine cornmeal

1 pint pistachio gelato or ice cream, softened

1 pint vanilla ice cream, softened

1 pint strawberry ice cream, softened

1¼ cups heavy cream

2 tablespoons confectioners' sugar, sifted

3 ounces small strawberries, hulled and sliced (about ½ cup), for serving

1 tablespoon chopped pistachios, for serving

**1.** Preheat oven to 350°F. Butter a 10-by-15-inch jelly-roll pan. Line with parchment, leaving a 2-inch overhang on short sides; butter parchment.

**2.** In a large bowl, whisk together butter, granulated sugar, and zest; whisk in eggs and salt. Add flour and cornmeal; whisk until just smooth. Spread batter evenly in pan. Bake until cake is dry to the touch and edges have begun to pull away from pan, about 15 minutes. Transfer pan to a wire rack to cool completely.

**3.** Using parchment overhang, remove cake from pan to a work surface, and cut into thirds, forming three 5-by-3-inch rectangles. Cover a rimmed baking sheet with a large sheet of plastic wrap; place a cake rectangle on it. Spread with pistachio gelato and freeze until firm, about 15 minutes. Top with second cake rectangle; spread with vanilla ice cream and return to freezer until firm, about 15 minutes. Top with third cake rectangle; spread with strawberry ice cream and freeze until firm, about 15 minutes. Wrap entire cake in plastic and freeze until ready to serve, up to 2 weeks.

**4.** Remove plastic and transfer cake to a serving dish. With an electric mixer on medium speed, beat heavy cream with confectioners' sugar until stiff peaks form. Frost cake with whipped cream. Freeze until firm, about 1 hour. Before serving, let cake stand at room temperature 10 minutes; then garnish top with strawberries and pistachios.

**BAKING TIP**

Beat the ice cream with an electric mixer on medium until pliable enough to spread.

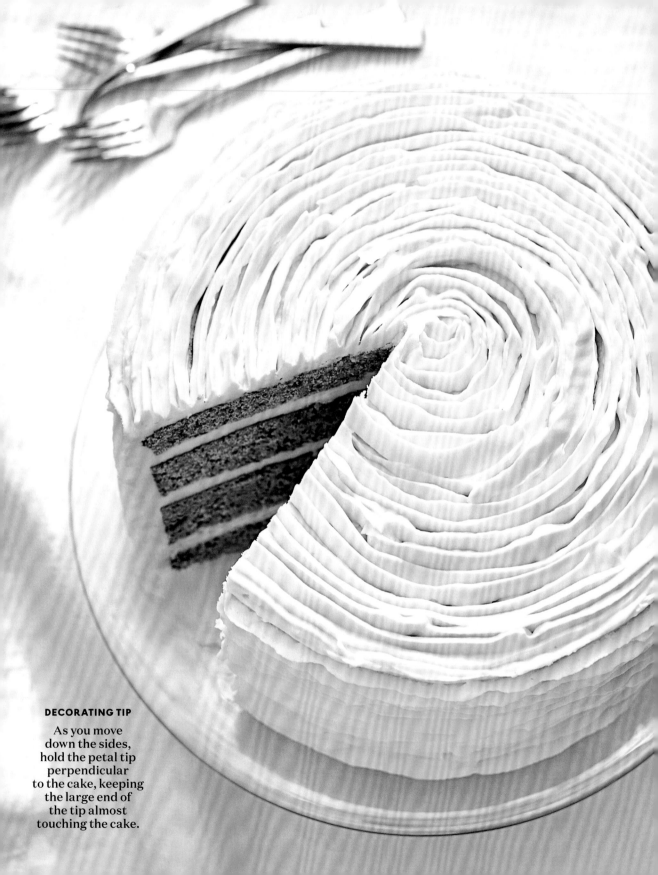

**DECORATING TIP**

As you move down the sides, hold the petal tip perpendicular to the cake, keeping the large end of the tip almost touching the cake.

# Carrot Cake with
# White Chocolate Frosting

**MAKES ONE 8-INCH LAYER CAKE**

*You can dress up a carrot cake in elegant ruffles using just a pastry bag
and a standard petal tip. Starting at the center of the cake and holding the
tip vertically, pipe the frosting while slowing turning the table or plate.
Gradually work outward and down the sides to create the swirling rose effect.*

---

2½ sticks (1¼ cups)
unsalted butter, melted,
plus more for pans

3 cups unbleached
all-purpose flour

1 tablespoon baking powder

1 teaspoon kosher salt

1½ teaspoons ground
cinnamon

2 teaspoons ground ginger

½ teaspoon freshly
grated nutmeg

5 medium carrots,
peeled and shredded
on the fine holes of
a box grater or food
processor (about 3 cups)

4 large eggs,
room temperature

1½ cups sugar

2 teaspoons vanilla extract

White Chocolate
Frosting (page 240)

**1.** Preheat oven to 350°F. Brush two 8-inch round cake pans with butter. Line with parchment; butter parchment. In a medium bowl, whisk together flour, baking powder, salt, cinnamon, ginger, and nutmeg. Transfer ½ cup of flour mixture to another medium bowl and toss with carrots to coat.

**2.** With an electric mixer on medium-high speed, beat eggs with sugar until pale and fluffy, about 5 minutes. While still beating, drizzle in butter, then beat in vanilla until combined. Reduce speed to low and add remaining flour mixture, beating just until combined. Fold flour-coated carrots into batter. Divide batter evenly between prepared pans, smoothing tops with an offset spatula.

**3.** Bake until a cake tester comes out clean, 33 to 37 minutes. Transfer pans to a wire rack to cool 10 minutes. Turn out cakes onto rack to cool completely.

**4.** With a serrated knife, trim tops of cake layers to level; split each cake in half horizontally to form a total of 4 layers. Place bottom layer of one cake, cut-side up, on a cake stand or a plate lined with parchment strips. Spread evenly with ¾ cup frosting. Top with other half of cake, cut-side down; spread evenly with another ¾ cup frosting. Repeat layering and frosting with second cake. Spread 1 cup frosting evenly over top and sides to create a crumb coat. Refrigerate, uncovered, until frosting is firm, at least 30 minutes.

**5.** Transfer remaining frosting to a pastry bag fitted with a petal tip (such as Ateco or Wilton #104). Starting at top center of cake and holding tip vertically, pipe frosting while slowly turning stand or plate, gradually working outward toward edges to create a swirl effect. Repeat process down side of cake, starting at top edge. (Cake can be stored, uncovered, at room temperature up to 12 hours or refrigerated, uncovered, up to 2 days; bring to room temperature before serving.)

# Naked Fruit Chiffon Cake

## MAKES ONE 9-INCH LAYER CAKE

*Are you confident enough to go naked? If you bake up an airy,
egg-white-lightened chiffon cake like this one, you should be! All these
romantic layers need are whipped cream and some gorgeous
in-season fruit, drizzled with a warm berry sauce—no frosting in sight.*

**FOR THE CAKE**

Unsalted butter, room
temperature, for pans

1¾ cups cake flour
(not self-rising)

1¼ cups sugar

1¾ teaspoons
baking powder

¾ teaspoon kosher salt

⅓ cup safflower oil

6 large egg yolks plus
8 large egg whites,
room temperature

⅔ cup whole milk

2 teaspoons lemon zest

1 vanilla bean, split
and seeds scraped

¼ teaspoon cream of tartar

Whipped Cream (page 242)

Seasonal fruit, such as
Seckel pears, figs, plums,
Concord grapes, and
blackberries, for garnish

**FOR THE BLACKBERRY
COULIS**

2 cups fresh blackberries

2 tablespoons sugar

2 tablespoons
fresh lemon juice

**1. Make the cake:** Preheat oven to 325°F. Butter two 9-inch round cake pans. Line with parchment; butter parchment. In a large bowl, whisk together flour, ¾ cup sugar, the baking powder, and salt.

**2.** In another large bowl, whisk together oil, egg yolks, milk, lemon zest, and vanilla seeds. Whisk egg yolk mixture into flour mixture.

**3.** With an electric mixer, whisk egg whites on high speed until frothy. Add cream of tartar and beat until soft peaks form, about 2 minutes. Gradually add remaining ½ cup sugar, beating until stiff, glossy peaks form, about 5 minutes. Whisk one-third of egg-white mixture into batter. Gently fold in remaining egg-white mixture with a rubber spatula. Divide batter evenly between prepared pans. Bake until golden and tops spring back when lightly touched, about 30 minutes. Transfer pans to a wire rack to cool 10 minutes. Turn out cakes upside down onto rack to cool completely.

**4. Make the blackberry coulis:** In a medium saucepan over medium-high heat, bring blackberries, sugar, lemon juice, and 2 tablespoons water to a boil. Reduce to a simmer for 5 minutes, stirring occasionally and breaking up berries with the back of a spoon. Pass berry mixture through a fine-mesh sieve, pressing on solids to release all juices. Let cool to room temperature.

**5.** With a serrated knife, trim tops of cake layers to level; split each in half horizontally to form a total of 4 layers. Place a layer, bottom-side down, on a serving platter. Spread 1½ cups whipped cream evenly over top. Repeat process with remaining cake layers, spreading 1½ cups whipped cream between each layer and leaving top layer uncovered. For stability, insert a wooden dowel or skewer into center of cake, trimmed so that the dowel is just shorter than top of cake. Spread remaining 1½ cups whipped cream over top of cake in decorative swirls. Garnish with fruit, scattering on top of cake and around perimeter of serving platter. Drizzle with coulis and serve immediately.

**BAKING TIP**

Adding a cup of the egg mixture to the brown butter (in step 4) helps prevent the eggs from deflating once the batter is thoroughly combined.

# Genoise with Cranberry Curd Filling

**MAKES ONE 8-INCH LAYER CAKE**

*A sweet-tart curd made with plump cranberries stars in this light, buttery French-style sponge cake. Though a genoise is traditionally served with fresh fruit, we opted to pair whipped cream with sugared cranberries, for a glistening effect. You can use fresh berries in fall or frozen when out of season.*

6 tablespoons unsalted butter, plus more for pan

2/3 cup cake flour (not self–rising), plus more for pan

1 teaspoon vanilla extract

5 large eggs, room temperature

1/2 cup plus 2 tablespoons superfine sugar

1/2 cup cornstarch

Cranberry Curd (page 233)

Whipped Cream (page 242)

Sugared Cranberries (page 245; optional)

**1.** Preheat oven to 350°F. Butter a 12½-by-17½-inch rimmed baking sheet. Line with parchment; butter parchment. Dust with flour, tapping out any excess.

**2.** In a small saucepan, melt butter over medium heat and cook, swirling pan occasionally, until golden brown, 3 to 5 minutes. Transfer brown butter to a large bowl; stir in vanilla and keep warm (110 to 120°F).

**3.** Fill a medium saucepan with a few inches of water and bring to a simmer. Lightly whisk together eggs and sugar in a heatproof bowl. Set bowl over (not in) simmering water, and whisk until superfine sugar is dissolved and mixture is warm to the touch, about 2 minutes.

**4.** With an electric mixer, whisk egg mixture on high speed until light and quadrupled in volume, at least 5 minutes. Whisk 1 cup egg mixture into warm butter mixture.

**5.** Sift together flour and cornstarch. Gently and quickly fold half the flour mixture into remaining egg mixture until combined, then repeat with remaining flour mixture. Gently fold in butter mixture. Pour batter into prepared pan, smoothing top with an offset spatula.

**6.** Bake until golden brown and edges begin to pull away from sides, 14 to 16 minutes. (Avoid opening oven door during baking, as cake is fragile and may collapse.) Transfer to a wire rack to cool completely.

**7.** With a serrated knife, cut cake in half lengthwise and widthwise to make 4 equal rectangles, each about 8 by 6 inches. Place a layer, bottom-side down, on a cake stand; spread a scant ½ cup curd evenly on top. Set another cake layer on top, and repeat process with remaining curd and cake layers. Refrigerate until firm, about 30 minutes. Spread a thin layer of frosting over cake to form a crumb coat; refrigerate until firm, about 30 minutes. Spread whipped cream evenly over top and sides of cakes. Top with sugared cranberries, if desired.

# Chocolate Pecan Guinness Caramel Cake

*Layers of chocolate stout cake are filled with buttercream, drizzled with salted caramel and chocolate ganache, then topped with addictively crunchy candied pecans. To keep all these luscious layers stable, insert a dowel through the center of the cake.*

---

### FOR THE CAKE

4 sticks (2 cups) unsalted butter, plus more for pans

1½ cups unsweetened Dutch-process cocoa powder, plus more for pans

2 cups Guinness or other stout

4 cups unbleached all-purpose flour

4 cups sugar

1 tablespoon baking soda

1½ teaspoons kosher salt

4 large eggs, room temperature

1⅓ cups sour cream or Greek yogurt

### FOR THE CANDIED PECANS

1 cup sugar

1½ cups (6 ounces) whole pecans or pecan pieces

### FOR THE SALTED CARAMEL

1 cup heavy cream

2 cups sugar

2 tablespoons light corn syrup

1 teaspoon kosher salt

1 stick (½ cup) unsalted butter, cut into tablespoons

### FOR THE CARAMEL BUTTERCREAM

1¼ cups sugar

5 large egg whites, room temperature

4 sticks (2 cups) unsalted butter, cut into tablespoons, room temperature

1 teaspoon vanilla extract

½ to ¾ cup salted caramel (recipe above)

### FOR THE CHOCOLATE GANACHE

6 ounces semisweet chocolate, coarsely chopped

¾ cup heavy cream

2 tablespoons butter, cut into small pieces, room temperature

**1. Make the cake:** Preheat oven to 350°F. Butter two 9-inch round cake pans. Line bottoms of pans with parchment; butter parchment. Dust pans with cocoa, tapping out any excess. In a large saucepan over medium heat, bring stout and butter to a simmer. Remove from heat; whisk in cocoa until smooth. Let cool completely.

**2.** In a large bowl, whisk together flour, sugar, baking soda, and salt. With an electric mixer, beat eggs and sour cream until combined. Add stout mixture and beat on low speed until combined; add flour mixture and beat until combined. Divide batter evenly between prepared pans, smoothing tops with an offset spatula.

**3.** Bake until tops spring back when lightly touched and a cake tester comes out with just a few crumbs attached, 35 to 45 minutes. Transfer pans to a wire rack to cool 10 minutes. Turn out cakes onto rack to cool completely.

*(continued on page 94)*

**4. Make the candied pecans:** Line a rimmed baking sheet with a non-stick baking mat. In a small saucepan, heat sugar and ¼ cup water over medium-high; cook, swirling occasionally, until sugar is dissolved and mixture is medium amber in color, 2 to 3 minutes. Remove from heat; immediately stir in pecans. Pour onto prepared sheet to cool completely. Transfer pecans to a cutting board and coarsely chop.

**5. Make the salted caramel:** In a small saucepan, heat cream over low. In a medium saucepan, stir together sugar, corn syrup, and ⅓ cup water; cook over medium-high, without stirring, until mixture is dark amber in color, about 15 minutes. Remove from heat; carefully pour in cream (mixture may splatter) and stir until smooth. Reduce heat to medium and cook until a candy thermometer reads 238°F (soft-ball stage), about 2 minutes. Pour mixture into a medium bowl; stir in salt. Let cool about 15 minutes, then stir in butter, 1 tablespoon at a time. Let cool completely.

**6. Make the caramel buttercream:** In a heatproof bowl, whisk together sugar and egg whites. Set over (not in) a pot of simmering water and whisk until sugar is dissolved and a thermometer registers 140°F. Remove bowl from heat. With an electric mixer on medium-high, whisk buttercream mixture until stiff, glossy peaks form. Reduce speed to medium-low and add butter, a few tablespoons at a time; continue beating until smooth. Stir in vanilla and caramel.

**7. Make the chocolate ganache:** Place chocolate in a medium bowl. In a small saucepan over medium, bring cream just to a boil. Pour over chocolate and let stand 1 minute. Stir until smooth and shiny, then stir in butter. Let cool 20 minutes.

**8. For assembly:** With a serrated knife, trim tops of cake layers to level; split each cake in half horizontally to form a total of 4 layers. Place a layer, bottom-side down, on a cake stand. Spread evenly with about 2 cups caramel buttercream, then sprinkle with some candied pecans. Drizzle with caramel and sprinkle with a few more candied pecans. Repeat process with remaining cake layers, leaving top layer (bottom-side up) uncovered. For stability, insert a dowel into center of cake, trimmed so that it's just shorter than top of cake. Spread ganache over top and sprinkle with remaining candied pecans. Refrigerate for 20 minutes before serving.

**STORAGE TIP**

This cake can be done in stages over time, at your convenience: The buttercream and chocolate ganache can be refrigerated, up to 3 days, or frozen, up to 1 month, in an airtight container, with plastic wrap pressed directly on surface. The candied pecans can be stored in an airtight container up to 2 weeks or in the freezer up to 1 month.

**BAKING TIP**

As an alternative,
you can use a 9-by-13-inch
pan; the baking time
will be about the same.

# Apple Layer Cake

**MAKES ONE 8-INCH LAYER CAKE**

*Apples take center stage in this delightfully spiced cake: Grated and diced pieces get folded into the batter, while baked slices (make them while the cake is chilling or up to two days ahead) adorn the cream cheese frosting. We fell in love with Pink-a-Boos at the farmers' market, but choose whatever baking apples catch your eye.*

**FOR THE CAKE**

1 stick (½ cup) unsalted butter, melted, plus more for pans

2 cups unbleached all-purpose flour, plus more for pans

2 teaspoons baking soda

½ teaspoon baking powder

2 teaspoons ground cinnamon

½ teaspoon ground ginger

¾ teaspoon kosher salt

2 cups packed light-brown sugar

2 large eggs, room temperature

4 small baking apples (about 20 ounces), such as Pink-a-Boos or Granny Smiths, peeled: 2 coarsely grated and 2 diced small

Cream Cheese Frosting (page 240)

**FOR THE APPLE CHIPS**

½ cup sugar

4 small baking apples (about 20 ounces), such as Pink-a-Boos or Granny Smiths, seeded and cut into ⅛- to ¼-inch-thick slices

**1. Make the cake:** Preheat oven to 350°F. Butter three 8-inch round cake pans. Line with parchment; butter parchment. Dust with flour, tapping out any excess. In a medium bowl, whisk together flour, baking soda, baking powder, cinnamon, ginger, and salt.

**2.** In a large bowl, whisk together butter, brown sugar, and eggs until well combined; fold in grated and diced apples. Add flour mixture and mix just until combined. Divide batter evenly among prepared pans, smoothing tops with an offset spatula.

**3.** Bake until a cake tester comes out clean, 35 to 40 minutes. Transfer pans to a wire rack to cool 20 minutes. Turn out cakes onto rack and cool completely. With a serrated knife, trim tops of cakes layers to level. Transfer a cake, trimmed-side up, to a cake plate or stand lined with parchment strips. Spread about 1 cup frosting evenly over it; top with a second cake layer. Repeat with another 1 cup frosting and third cake layer. Spread a thin layer of frosting over cake to form a crumb coat; refrigerate until firm, about 30 minutes. Spread remaining frosting evenly over top and sides of cake. Refrigerate at least 1 hour and up to 4 days.

**4. Make the baked apple chips:** Decrease oven to 225°F. In a medium saucepan, bring sugar and ½ cup water to a boil over medium-high heat, stirring occasionally to dissolve sugar. Working in batches, cook apple slices until just translucent and barely tender, 30 seconds to 1 minute. Transfer slices to 2 parchment-lined baking sheets, spaced ½- to 1-inch apart. Transfer to oven and dry until apples are slightly firm, 1½ to 2½ hours, flipping slices every 30 minutes. Transfer to a wire rack to cool completely and dry. (Apple chips can be stored in an airtight container up to 2 days.)

**5.** Bring cake to room temperature. Decorate base of cake with apple chips, overlapping slightly. Use a serrated knife to slice cake and serve.

# Mile-High Salted-Caramel Chocolate Cake

**MAKES ONE 9-INCH LAYER CAKE**

*Truly, madly, and deeply chocolate: Pools of rich salted caramel separate layers of chocolate cake, which are then swathed with dark chocolate frosting and sprinkled with flaky salt. Prep the wondrous cake layers and caramel up to three days before assembling (chilling actually improves the texture for stacking), so you can make it look effortless.*

---

**FOR THE CAKE**

Unsalted butter, room temperature, for pans

1½ cups unsweetened Dutch-process cocoa powder,

3 cups unbleached all-purpose flour

3 cups sugar

1 tablespoon baking soda

1½ teaspoons baking powder

1½ teaspoons kosher salt

4 large eggs, room temperature

1½ cups buttermilk

1½ cups warm water

½ cup plus 2 tablespoons safflower oil

2 teaspoons vanilla extract

**FOR THE CARAMEL**

4 cups sugar

¼ cup light corn syrup

2 cups heavy cream

1 teaspoon kosher salt

2 sticks (1 cup) cold unsalted butter, cut into tablespoons

Double Chocolate Frosting (page 241)

Flaky sea salt, such as Maldon, for sprinkling

**1. Make the cake:** Preheat oven to 350°F. Butter three 9-inch round cake pans. Line with parchment; butter parchment. Dust with cocoa, tapping out any excess. In a large bowl, whisk together flour, sugar, cocoa, baking soda, baking powder, and salt with an electric mixer on low speed until just combined. Increase speed to medium and add eggs, buttermilk, warm water, oil, and vanilla; beat until smooth, about 3 minutes.

**2.** Divide batter evenly among prepared pans, smoothing tops with an offset spatula. Bake until cakes are set and a cake tester comes out clean, about 35 minutes. Transfer pans to a wire rack to cool 15 minutes. Turn out cakes onto rack to cool completely.

**3. Make the caramel:** In a medium saucepan over high heat, combine sugar, corn syrup, and ¼ cup water. Cook, without stirring, until mixture is dark amber, about 14 minutes. Remove from heat and carefully pour in cream (mixture will spatter); stir until smooth. Return to high heat and cook until a candy thermometer reaches 238°F, soft-ball stage, about 2 minutes. Pour caramel into a medium bowl, stir in salt, and let cool slightly, about 15 minutes. Stir in butter, 1 tablespoon at a time. Let cool completely.

**4.** With a serrated knife, trim tops of cake layers to level; split each in half horizontally to form a total of 6 layers. Transfer a layer to a serving plate or cake stand lined with parchment strips, and spread ¾ cup caramel over top. Top with another cake layer, and repeat with remaining caramel and cake layers, leaving top layer uncovered. Refrigerate until set, about 1 hour. Spread a thin layer of frosting over cake to form a crumb coat; refrigerate until firm, about 30 minutes. Spread frosting evenly over top and sides of cake in a swirling, swooping motion. Sprinkle with sea salt.

**DECORATING TIP**

When assembling the icebox cake, anchor the initial four corner cookies to the platter with a dab of whipped cream, to help stabilize the shape.

# Mint-Chocolate Icebox Cake

MAKES ONE 8-INCH LAYER CAKE

*Get the whole family involved in constructing this dessert,*
*as building the cookie layers speaks to the kids, while the mint-chocolate flavor*
*beckons us all. The cake starts out sturdy*
*and then softens in the refrigerator into sliceable pieces of heaven.*

---

**FOR THE COOKIES**

4½ cups unbleached
all-purpose flour,
plus more for dusting

1¾ cups unsweetened
Dutch-process cocoa powder

¾ teaspoon kosher salt

4½ sticks (2¼ cups)
unsalted butter,
room temperature

3¾ cups confectioners'
sugar, sifted

3 large eggs,
room temperature

1½ teaspoons vanilla extract

**FOR THE MINT
WHIPPED CREAM**

2¼ cups heavy cream

¼ cup confectioners'
sugar, sifted

¼ teaspoon mint extract

Dark chocolate, for garnish

**1. Make the cookies:** Whisk together flour, cocoa, and salt in a large bowl.

**2.** With an electric mixer, beat butter and confectioners' sugar on medium-high speed until fluffy, 3 to 5 minutes, scraping down sides of bowl as needed. Add eggs, one at a time, beating well after each addition; add vanilla. Reduce speed to low and gradually add flour mixture, beating until well combined.

**3.** Divide dough into quarters. Between sheets of parchment, roll dough to a scant ¼-inch thick. Refrigerate until chilled, at least 30 minutes and up to 1 hour.

**4.** Preheat oven to 350°F. Working in batches, cut dough into squares using a 2½-inch cutter, rerolling scraps once as necessary (you will need a total of 63 cookies). Transfer to parchment-lined baking sheets; refrigerate until firm, at least 15 minutes. Bake until cookies are just firm to the touch but not dark, 10 to 12 minutes. Transfer cookies on sheets to wire racks to cool.

**5. Make the mint whipped cream:** In a large bowl, whisk heavy cream, confectioners' sugar, and mint extract, on medium-high speed to stiff peaks.

**6.** On a platter, arrange 9 cookies into a square, with edges touching. Evenly spread ¾ cup mint whipped cream over cookies. Repeat layers five more times, topping with a final layer of cookies. Wrap loosely with plastic. Transfer to refrigerator to chill for at least 4 hours and up to 12 hours. Before serving, shave dark chocolate over the top with a handheld grater.

# 3

# Everyday Cakes

*These are kick-off-your-shoes, weekday-baking, anytime cakes. They indulge our childlike love for snickerdoodles and PB&Js while playing to our grown-up tastes for bourbon and berries and all kinds of buttery goodness. They have a way of making the everyday extraordinary.*

———

# Pistachio-Cardamom Bundt

**SERVES 10 TO 14**

*Fragrant with spice and colorful with Sicilian pistachios and dried rose petals, this Bundt cake nods to the Middle East. We chose to decorate with rose petals, but also consider organic fresh chamomile or elderflower. The trickiest part of any Bundt is getting it out of the pan in one piece—so butter generously then sprinkle with flour.*

## FOR THE CAKE

2 sticks (1 cup) unsalted butter, room temperature, plus more for pan

2¼ cups unbleached all-purpose flour, plus more for pan

1 cup shelled unsalted pistachios, preferably Sicilian

1 teaspoon baking powder

½ teaspoon baking soda

1 teaspoon kosher salt

½ teaspoon ground cardamom

1½ cups granulated sugar

4 large eggs, room temperature

1 cup buttermilk, room temperature

## FOR THE GLAZE

2 cups confectioners' sugar, sifted

¼ teaspoon rose water

2 to 3 tablespoons whole milk

¼ cup shelled unsalted pistachios, preferably Sicilian, finely chopped

3 tablespoons dried organic rose petals

**1. Make the cake:** Preheat oven to 350°F with rack in center. Using a pastry brush, generously butter a 12-cup Bundt pan; dust with flour, tapping out any excess. Pulse pistachios in a food processor until finely ground. In a medium bowl, whisk together ground pistachios, flour, baking powder, baking soda, salt, and cardamom.

**2.** In a large bowl, with an electric mixer, beat butter and sugar on medium-high until light and fluffy, about 3 minutes, scraping down sides of bowl as needed. Add eggs, one at a time, beating well after each addition. Reduce speed to low and add flour mixture in two batches, alternating with buttermilk.

**3.** Pour batter into prepared pan and bake until it springs back to touch and a cake tester comes out clean, 45 to 50 minutes. Transfer pan to a wire rack set on a baking sheet or a piece of parchment to cool 30 minutes. Turn out cake onto rack to cool completely.

**4. Make the glaze:** In a medium bowl, whisk together confectioners' sugar, rose water, and milk until smooth. (For a glaze that is more opaque, use less milk, and for a thinner glaze, use a bit more.) Transfer glaze to a measuring cup, and pour over top of cake in a circular motion. Sprinkle with pistachios and rose petals immediately. Let set for 30 minutes before slicing.

**BAKING TIP**
Toast the coconut in a 350°F oven for 5 to 10 minutes, stirring often. Keep a constant eye on it, as coconut can quickly go from browned to burned.

# Tropical Pound Cake

SERVES 8

*Tangy buttermilk balances the sumptuously sweet coconut—
which gets baked inside and then sprinkled on top for
good measure—in this family favorite. Toast the coconut
before you begin to bake, up to a day ahead.*

1½ sticks (¾ cup)
unsalted butter,
room temperature,
plus more for pan

2 cups unbleached
all-purpose flour,
plus more for pan

½ teaspoon
baking powder

1 teaspoon kosher salt

1 cup granulated sugar

1 teaspoon vanilla extract

3 large eggs,
room temperature

1 cup plus 2 tablespoons
buttermilk

1½ cups sweetened
shredded coconut, toasted

1 cup confectioners'
sugar, sifted

**1.** Preheat oven to 350°F. Butter a 4½-by-8½-inch loaf pan; dust with flour, tapping out any excess. In a medium bowl, whisk together flour, baking powder, and salt. In a large bowl, beat butter and granulated sugar with an electric mixer on medium-high speed until light and fluffy, scraping down sides of bowl as needed. Add vanilla and then eggs, one at a time, beating well and scraping down sides of bowl as needed. Reduce speed to low, add flour mixture in three batches, alternating with two ½-cup additions of buttermilk, and beat until combined. With a rubber spatula, fold in 1¼ cups coconut.

**2.** Transfer batter to prepared pan and bake until golden and a cake tester comes out with a few moist crumbs attached, about 1 hour. Transfer pan to a wire rack set in a rimmed baking sheet and turn out cake on rack to cool completely. (Store at room temperature, wrapped in plastic, up to 4 days.)

**3.** Whisk together confectioners' sugar and remaining 2 tablespoons buttermilk. Drizzle over cake and sprinkle with remaining ¼ cup coconut.

# Nectarine Skillet Cake

## SERVES 8

*Thin slices of the stone fruit play the part of rose petals atop an easy skillet cake that proves delightfully both rustic and elegant. Beginning on the outer edge of the pan, place the nectarine slices skin-side up, overlapping slightly, to form concentric circles until arriving at the bud-like center.*

4 tablespoons
unsalted butter,
room temperature,
plus more for pan

1 cup unbleached
all-purpose flour

½ teaspoon baking powder

¼ teaspoon baking soda

½ teaspoon kosher salt

¾ cup plus
3 tablespoons sugar

1 large egg,
room temperature

2 teaspoons vanilla extract

½ cup buttermilk,
room temperature

3 to 4 medium
nectarines, halved,
pitted, and thinly sliced

**1.** Preheat oven to 375°F. Butter an 8-inch cast-iron or enameled cast-iron pan. In a small bowl, combine flour, baking powder, baking soda, and salt.

**2.** In a medium bowl, beat butter and ¾ cup sugar with an electric mixer on medium-high speed until light and fluffy, about 2 minutes. Add egg and vanilla, and mix to combine. Add flour mixture in batches, alternating with buttermilk, and mix until batter is smooth.

**3.** Pour batter into skillet, spreading it evenly to the edges with a small offset spatula. Arrange nectarine slices, skin-side up, in concentric circles, beginning at the outer edge and ending in the center and overlapping slices as you go around. You should have a pattern that resembles a rose. Sprinkle with remaining 3 tablespoons sugar.

**4.** Bake until golden and a cake tester comes out clean, about 45 minutes. Let cool completely. Serve from the skillet.

# Fudgy Brownie Cake

### SERVES 10 TO 12

*Beneath its modest exterior, unadorned but for a dusting
of cocoa powder, this cake is so intensely flavored
that chocolate lovers will be hooked. That you can assemble it in
twenty minutes is all the icing you'll need.*

1 stick (½ cup) unsalted
butter, cut into tablespoons,
plus more for pan

¼ cup unsweetened
Dutch-process cocoa powder,
plus more for dusting

6 ounces bittersweet
chocolate
(61 to 70% cacao),
finely chopped

¾ cup plus
2 tablespoons sugar

1 large egg yolk plus
3 large egg whites,
room temperature

½ teaspoon kosher salt

3 tablespoons unbleached
all-purpose flour

**1.** Preheat oven to 325°F. Butter a 9-inch springform pan. Dust with cocoa, tapping out any excess. Melt butter and bittersweet chocolate in a heatproof bowl set over (not in) a saucepan of simmering water, stirring until smooth. Remove from heat and whisk in ¾ cup sugar. Whisk in egg yolk, then cocoa and salt.

**2.** In a medium bowl, beat egg whites with an electric mixer on medium speed until foamy. Increase speed to medium-high, gradually mixing in remaining 2 tablespoons sugar, and beat until stiff, glossy peaks form, about 4 minutes.

**3.** Fold flour into chocolate mixture with a rubber spatula, then fold in egg whites. Pour batter into pan, and spread evenly to edges with a small offset spatula. Bake until set, 30 to 35 minutes. Transfer pan to a wire rack to cool completely. Remove sides of pan and dust top of cake with cocoa. (Cake can be stored in pan at room temperature, wrapped in plastic wrap—but do not let plastic touch cake—up to 1 day.)

# Apricot Cheesecake

### SERVES 10

*Creamy cheesecake meets the perfect counterpoint in sweet-tart apricot. Blended with gelatin, fruit preserves form a translucent top layer that offers the golden glow of stained glass. To ensure a smooth texture, bloom the gelatin first: Sprinkle the powder over some water and let it stand for about five minutes.*

---

**FOR THE CRUST**

8 graham cracker sheets (about 5 ounces), finely ground (1 cup)

2 tablespoons unsalted butter, melted

2 tablespoons sugar

Pinch of kosher salt

**FOR THE FILLING**

4 packages (8 ounces each) cream cheese, room temperature

1½ cups plus 2 tablespoons sugar

Pinch of kosher salt

1 teaspoon vanilla extract

4 large eggs, room temperature

**FOR THE TOPPING**

½ teaspoon unflavored gelatin (from one ¼-ounce envelope)

1½ teaspoons cold water

One 13-ounce jar (1 cup plus 2 tablespoons) apricot preserves

**1. Make the crust:** Preheat oven to 350°F. Line the bottom of a 9-inch springform pan with a parchment round. In a medium bowl, stir together graham cracker crumbs, melted butter, sugar, and salt. Press crumb mixture firmly onto bottom of pan. Bake until set, about 10 minutes. Transfer pan to a wire rack to cool completely.

**2. Make the filling:** Reduce oven to 325°F. Wrap the exterior of the springform pan with a double layer of foil. Bring a kettle of water to boil. With an electric mixer, beat cream cheese on medium speed until fluffy and smooth, about 3 minutes. Reduce speed to low; add sugar in a slow, steady stream. Add salt and vanilla; beat until well combined. Add eggs, one at a time, beating after each addition until just combined (do not overmix).

**3.** Place springform pan in a large, shallow roasting pan. Pour filling into crust. Transfer pan to oven and carefully pour enough boiling water into roasting pan to reach halfway up sides of springform pan. Bake until cake is set but still slightly wobbly in center, about 1 hour 15 minutes.

**4.** Transfer pan to a wire rack and remove foil; let cool completely. Refrigerate, uncovered, at least 24 hours. Run a knife around edge of cake to loosen before unmolding.

**5. Make the topping:** In a small bowl, sprinkle gelatin over cold water. Let stand until softened, about 5 minutes. Meanwhile, in a small saucepan, heat apricot preserves over medium-low until warm, about 2 minutes. Add softened gelatin and stir to combine. Let cool slightly and then strain through a fine-mesh sieve over cheesecake. Spread evenly with an offset spatula and chill to set, about 2 hours, before serving.

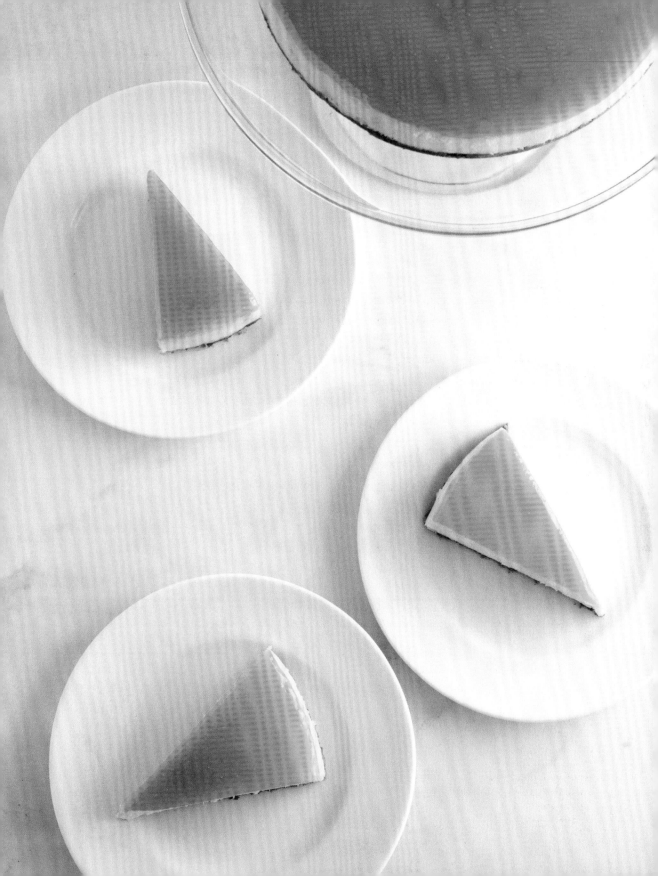

**BAKING TIP**
Rosy-red rhubarb
varieties like
New Valentine, which
Martha grows,
promise greater
sweetness.

# Rhubarb Crumb Cake

**SERVES 8**

*Rhubarb may be called pieplant, but we think its tart, juicy stalks
take the cake—especially when dotted with a crunchy
brown sugar crumble. But why stop there? Whisk the extra rhubarb syrup
from step 1 into whipped cream to bring it over the top.*

8 ounces rhubarb (about 3 stalks), halved lengthwise and cut into 3-inch pieces

1 cup granulated sugar

1¾ cups unbleached all-purpose flour, plus more for pan

½ cup packed light-brown sugar

¾ teaspoon kosher salt

4 tablespoons cold unsalted butter, cut into small pieces, plus 6 tablespoons room-temperature butter, plus more for pan

1¼ teaspoons baking powder

2 large eggs, room temperature

¼ cup sour cream, room temperature

1 teaspoon grated orange zest

1 cup heavy cream

**1.** In a medium bowl, toss rhubarb with ¼ cup granulated sugar. Let stand, tossing occasionally, until sugar is dissolved, about 30 minutes.

**2. Make the streusel:** In a medium bowl, stir together ½ cup flour, the brown sugar, and ¼ teaspoon salt. Using your fingers, cut in cold butter until medium clumps form. Press mixture into bottom of bowl; refrigerate until ready to use, at least 20 minutes.

**3.** Preheat oven to 350°F. Butter a 9-inch round cake pan. Line with parchment; butter parchment. Dust with flour, tapping out any excess. In a medium bowl, whisk together baking powder and remaining 1¼ cups flour and ½ teaspoon salt. In another medium bowl, stir together room-temperature butter and remaining ¾ cup sugar. Whisk in eggs, one at a time. Fold in half of flour mixture, then sour cream and zest. Stir in remaining flour mixture just to combine. Transfer batter to prepared pan, smoothing top with an offset spatula.

**4.** Break streusel into large pieces; sprinkle half over batter. Strain rhubarb (reserving syrup); scatter over batter, then top with remaining streusel. Bake until cake pulls away from sides of pan and a cake tester comes out clean, 40 to 45 minutes. Transfer pan to a wire rack to cool 20 minutes. Turn out cake onto rack to cool completely.

**5.** Whip cream to soft peaks; then sweeten to taste with reserved rhubarb syrup. Whisk until soft peaks return and serve with cake.

# Red Velvet Pound Cake

### SERVES 12

*When you need a make-ahead dessert that tastes like it just popped out of the oven, this deeply satisfying pound cake does the trick. Buttermilk is the secret weapon that keeps it velvety for up to two days.*

---

1 stick (½ cup) plus 2 tablespoons unsalted butter, room temperature, plus more for pan

2 tablespoons unsweetened Dutch-process cocoa powder, plus more for pan

1½ cups unbleached all-purpose flour

¼ teaspoon baking soda

1 teaspoon kosher salt

1¼ cups granulated sugar

3 large eggs, room temperature

¾ teaspoon vanilla extract

½ teaspoon distilled white vinegar

½ cup buttermilk, room temperature

¼ teaspoon gel-paste food coloring in red

4 ounces cream cheese, room temperature

½ cup confectioners' sugar, sifted

**1.** Preheat oven to 325°F. Butter a 9-by-5-inch loaf pan. Dust with cocoa, tapping out any excess. In a medium bowl, whisk together flour, cocoa, baking soda, and salt.

**2.** In a separate medium bowl, beat butter and granulated sugar with an electric mixer on high speed until pale and fluffy, about 4 minutes. Scrape down sides of bowl as needed. Reduce speed to medium; add eggs, one at a time, beating well after each addition and scraping down sides of bowl as needed. Beat in ½ teaspoon vanilla and the vinegar. Reduce speed to low; add flour mixture in three batches, alternating with buttermilk and beginning and ending with flour mixture, until just combined. Add gel; beat until fully incorporated.

**3.** Pour batter into prepared pan. Tap pan on counter and smooth top with an offset spatula. Bake until a cake tester comes out clean, about 1 hour 20 minutes, tenting with foil if browning too quickly. Transfer pan to a wire rack to cool for 15 minutes. Turn out cake onto rack to cool completely. (Cake can be stored, wrapped in plastic, at room temperature up to 2 days.)

**4.** When ready to serve, beat cream cheese with confectioners' sugar and remaining ¼ teaspoon vanilla in a medium bowl and with an electric mixer on medium-high speed until smooth. Spread evenly over top of cake with an offset spatula. Slice cake and serve.

# Double-Orange Bundt Cake

**SERVES 10 TO 12**

*This Bundt bursts with a double dose of orange: Fresh juice and zest get mixed into the batter, while a Cointreau-spiked syrup is soaked into the bottom and then brushed on top for a crackly glaze. We used Nordic Ware's Brilliance Bundt pan for this beautiful sunburst design, but any 10-cup shape will work.*

---

**FOR THE CAKE**

2 sticks (1 cup) unsalted butter, room temperature, plus more for pan

3 cups unbleached all-purpose flour, plus more for pan

½ cup whole milk

1 tablespoon grated orange zest plus ½ cup fresh juice (from 2 large oranges)

1 teaspoon baking powder

¾ teaspoon baking soda

1½ teaspoons kosher salt

1¼ teaspoons ground cardamom

1½ cups sugar

4 large eggs, room temperature

1 tablespoon vanilla extract

**FOR THE GLAZE**

1 stick (½ cup) unsalted butter

½ cup orange liqueur, such as Cointreau or triple sec

⅔ cup sugar

**1. Make the cake:** Preheat oven to 350°F. Generously brush a 10- to 15-cup Bundt pan with butter; dust with flour, tapping out excess. In a small bowl, stir together milk and orange juice. In another bowl, whisk together flour, baking powder, baking soda, salt, and cardamom to thoroughly combine.

**2.** With an electric mixer, beat butter with sugar and orange zest on medium-high speed in a large bowl until pale and fluffy, 2 to 3 minutes. Beat in eggs, one at a time, then vanilla. Reduce speed to medium-low and beat in flour mixture in two additions, alternating with milk mixture, and beginning and ending with flour, just until combined. Transfer batter to prepared pan, smoothing top with an offset spatula.

**3.** Bake until cake is puffed slightly and a wooden skewer inserted into center comes out clean, about 45 minutes. Let cool in pan on a wire rack 15 minutes (do not turn off oven).

**4. Make the glaze:** In a small saucepan, cook butter over medium-high heat until boiling. Remove from heat; carefully add liqueur (mixture will bubble). When bubbles subside, stir in sugar. Return to medium-low heat and cook, stirring, until sugar has dissolved, about 1 minute. Remove from heat.

**5.** Pierce holes in cake with skewer at 1-inch intervals. Brush half of glaze evenly over cake; let stand until fully absorbed, about 10 minutes. Invert cake onto a baking sheet. Brush remaining glaze evenly over top and sides.

**6.** Return to oven and bake just until glaze is set and dry, about 5 minutes. Transfer to rack and let cool completely before slicing and serving. (Glazed cake can be stored in an airtight container at room temperature for up to 3 days.)

# Bourbon and Berry Brown-Sugar Cake

### SERVES 8 TO 10

*When brown sugar and bourbon pair up, a rich caramel flavor and a tender crumb result. Plump berries offer a sweet touch (or try sour cherries, pitted and tossed with two tablespoons of sugar, for a tart taste), while a dollop of whipped cream seals the deal.*

---

1 stick (½ cup) unsalted butter, room temperature, plus more for pan

1¾ cups unbleached all-purpose flour

1¾ teaspoons baking powder

¾ teaspoon kosher salt

⅓ cup granulated sugar

⅔ cup packed light-brown sugar

2 large eggs, room temperature

4 teaspoons bourbon, such as Maker's Mark

⅔ cup whole milk, room temperature

1 cup raspberries

1 cup blueberries

Fine sanding sugar, for sprinkling

Whipped Cream (page 242), for serving

**1.** Preheat oven to 350°F. Butter a 9-inch round cake pan. Line with parchment; butter parchment. In a medium bowl, whisk together flour, baking powder, and salt.

**2.** In a large bowl, beat butter and both sugars with an electric mixer on medium-high speed until light and creamy, 2 to 3 minutes. Add eggs, one at a time, beating well after each addition. Beat in bourbon. Add flour mixture in three batches, alternating with milk and beginning and ending with flour; beat until just combined.

**3.** Transfer batter to prepared pan, smoothing top with an offset spatula. Sprinkle top with both berries, pressing some into batter. Sprinkle generously with sanding sugar. Bake until edges begin to pull away from pan and top springs back when lightly touched, 50 minutes to 1 hour. Transfer pan to a wire rack to cool 20 minutes. Turn out cake carefully (cake is quite fragile when warm) onto rack to cool completely, about 1 hour. Serve with whipped cream.

# Marble Pound Cake

### SERVES 8 TO 10

*Three curvy tiers of pound cake—dark chocolate, a lighter cocoa middle, and buttery vanilla—owe their tenderness to reverse creaming. The method, which entails mixing the butter with the dry ingredients before adding the eggs inhibits gluten from forming as the cake bakes, resulting in a velvety crumb.*

2 sticks (1 cup) plus 2 tablespoons unsalted butter, cut into pieces, room temperature, plus more for pan

3 large eggs, room temperature, whisked

⅓ cup whole milk, room temperature

2 teaspoons vanilla extract

1 cup plus 2 tablespoons sugar

1¾ cups unbleached all-purpose flour

1¼ teaspoons baking powder

1 teaspoon kosher salt

3 tablespoons unsweetened Dutch-process cocoa powder

4 ounces semisweet chocolate, melted and cooled

**1.** Preheat oven to 325°F. Butter a 9-by-5-inch loaf pan. In a medium bowl, whisk together eggs, milk, and vanilla. In a large bowl, beat together sugar, flour, baking powder, and salt with an electric mixer on low speed until just combined. Continue beating while adding butter, a piece at a time, until mixture is crumbly. Add half the milk mixture and beat on medium-high until fluffy, about 1 minute. Add remaining milk mixture and beat just until incorporated, about 30 seconds.

**2.** In another large bowl, whisk 2 tablespoons cocoa into melted chocolate. Stir in 1½ cups batter. Spoon into prepared pan, smoothing top with a small offset spatula. Whisk remaining 1 tablespoon cocoa into another 1½ cups batter in bowl; spoon over dark chocolate layer and smooth top. Spoon in remaining plain batter; smooth top.

**3.** Bake until cake springs back when lightly pressed or a cake tester comes out clean, about 1 hour 30 minutes (if top is browning too quickly, tent with foil). Transfer pan to a wire rack to cool 15 minutes. Turn out cake onto rack to cool completely. (Serve or wrap slices individually in plastic and freeze in bags for up to 3 months.)

# Flourless Chocolate Date Cake

SERVES 10 TO 12

*If a cake can be called sultry, this ultrarich chocolate dessert is that and more. Plump, juicy, amazingly sweet Medjool dates make it so; they're known as the "king of dates" for a reason. A warm caramel glaze sprinkled with flaky salt adds a high-sweet note to the richness that lies beneath.*

**FOR THE DATE PURÉE**

10 ounces Medjool dates, pitted

⅔ cup bourbon

**FOR THE CAKE**

1½ sticks (¾ cup) unsalted butter, room temperature, plus more, for pan

Unsweetened Dutch–process cocoa powder, for pan

12 ounces bittersweet chocolate (70% cacao), chopped

6 large eggs, separated, room temperature

¼ teaspoon kosher salt

½ teaspoon ground cinnamon

¼ cup sugar

**FOR THE CARAMEL**

1 cup sugar

⅓ cup heavy cream

**FOR SERVING**

1 teaspoon flaky sea salt, such as Maldon

Whipped Cream (page 242)

**1. Make the date purée:** In a small saucepan over medium-low heat, bring dates and bourbon to a simmer. Cook until almost all the liquid is absorbed. Remove from heat; cover and let cool. Purée in a food processor until smooth. (You should have about 1 cup.)

**2. Make the cake:** Preheat oven to 325°F. Butter a 9-inch springform pan. Line bottom with parchment; butter parchment. Dust pan with cocoa, tapping out any excess.

**3.** In a heatproof bowl set over (not in) a pan of simmering water, melt butter and chocolate, whisking until smooth. Remove from heat. Whisk in ⅔ cup date purée. Let cool; whisk in yolks, kosher salt, and cinnamon.

**4.** With an electric mixer on medium-high speed, whisk egg whites until soft peaks form, about 2 minutes. Slowly add sugar, beating until stiff, glossy peaks form. Fold one-third of whites into chocolate mixture, then fold in remaining whites. Transfer to prepared pan, smoothing top with an offset spatula. Bake until set (it should be cracking a bit on edges and shiny in center), about 30 minutes. Transfer pan to a wire rack to cool completely. Run a paring knife around sides of pan; remove from pan.

**5. Make the caramel:** In a small saucepan over medium-high heat, bring sugar and ¼ cup water to a boil, stirring until sugar is dissolved, about 2 minutes. Let boil, without stirring, until deep golden brown, swirling pan to color evenly, and washing down sides of pan with a wet pastry brush to keep crystals from forming, 10 to 11 minutes. Remove from heat; carefully pour in cream (it will spatter), stirring to combine. Stir in remaining ⅓ cup date purée. Pass caramel through a fine sieve to remove lumps. Let cool until thick but pourable, about 30 minutes.

**6.** Pour caramel over cake and spread with an offset spatula so it drips over sides. Sprinkle with flaky salt. Cut into wedges with a hot knife. Serve with whipped cream.

# Lemon Olive-Oil Cake

## SERVES 10 TO 12

*Olive oil ups the ante for a moist cake that actually improves the day after it's baked. It's the Mediterranean way, as is the bright lemon that will transport you to its sunny coasts. Serve it plain, sprinkled with confectioners' sugar, or with macerated berries and whipped mascarpone cream, as we do here.*

---

### FOR THE CAKE

¾ cup extra-virgin olive oil, plus more for pan

1½ cups unbleached all-purpose flour

½ teaspoon baking powder

1¼ teaspoons kosher salt

2 teaspoons finely grated lemon zest plus 3 tablespoons fresh juice

5 large eggs, separated and room temperature

⅓ cup plus ¾ cup granulated sugar

Confectioners' sugar, sifted, for dusting

### FOR THE BERRIES AND CREAM

4 cups fresh berries, such as raspberries, blueberries, and halved (or quartered, if large) strawberries

¼ cup granulated sugar

1 tablespoon fresh lemon juice

2 cups heavy cream

8 ounces mascarpone, stirred until smooth

**1. Make the cake:** Preheat oven to 350°F. Brush a 9-inch springform pan with olive oil and line bottom with a parchment round; oil parchment. Whisk together flour, baking powder, salt, and lemon zest in a medium bowl.

**2.** In a large bowl, with an electric mixer, whisk egg whites on medium-low speed until foamy. Increase speed to medium-high; slowly add ⅓ cup granulated sugar, beating just until whites hold soft peaks, 3 to 4 minutes. In another large bowl, with an electric mixer on medium-high speed, beat egg yolks with remaining ¾ cup granulated sugar until thick, pale, and tripled in volume, 2 to 3 minutes. Slowly beat in oil, then lemon juice to combine (mixture may appear curdled). Stir in flour mixture just to combine. Gently stir one-third of egg-white mixture into yolk mixture to lighten, then gently fold in remaining egg-white mixture until no streaks of white remain (do not overmix). Transfer batter to prepared pan; gently smooth top with an offset spatula.

**3.** Bake until cake is golden brown on top and springs back when lightly pressed, 45 to 55 minutes. Transfer pan to a wire rack to cool 15 minutes. Run a knife between sides of cake and pan to loosen. Remove sides of pan; let cool completely on rack.

**4. Make the berries and cream:** In a medium bowl, stir together berries, 2 tablespoons granulated sugar, and the lemon juice. Let stand at least 30 minutes and up to 2 hours. In another medium bowl, using an electric mixer, whisk cream until thick and silky but not holding peaks. Add mascarpone and remaining 2 tablespoons granulated sugar. Whisk just until soft peaks form.

**5.** Dust top of cake generously with confectioners' sugar. Serve with macerated berries and whipped mascarpone cream. (Cake can be made ahead and stored in an airtight container at room temperature up to 2 days.)

# Plum Upside-Down Cake

**SERVES 8**

*The beauty of this cake lies in both its caramelized fruit and artful
look when it's inverted after baking. When forming
the concentric circles of fruit, shingle the just-ripe plum slices as closely
as possible, because they will bake down in the oven.*

1½ sticks (¾ cup) unsalted
butter, room temperature

¾ cup packed
light–brown sugar

5 to 7 plums (depending
on size), halved and pitted

1 cup granulated sugar

2 large eggs, separated,
room temperature

1 teaspoon vanilla extract

1½ cups unbleached
all–purpose flour

2 teaspoons baking powder

1 teaspoon kosher salt

½ cup buttermilk,
room temperature

**1.** Preheat oven to 350°F. In a 10-inch cast-iron skillet, melt 4 tablespoons butter and the brown sugar over low heat. Using a fork, mix together until smooth. Remove pan from heat.

**2.** Place plum halves, cut-side down, on work surface, and cut into ¼-inch-thick slices. Transfer each slice, skin-side down, to skillet, in a concentric circle, beginning at the outer edge, ending in the center, and overlapping slices as you go around.

**3.** With an electric mixer, beat remaining 1 stick butter and the granulated sugar until light and fluffy. In a small bowl, beat egg yolks and vanilla; add to butter mixture. In another small bowl, whisk flour, baking powder, and salt. With mixer on low, add flour mixture, alternating with buttermilk and beginning and ending with flour mixture; beat until just combined. Transfer batter to a wide bowl.

**4.** With a clean electric mixer, whisk egg whites until soft peaks form, about 2 minutes. Stir one-third of egg whites into batter. Gently fold in remaining egg whites until incorporated. Pour batter over plums, spreading to cover evenly with an offset spatula.

**5.** Bake until top is browned and springs back when lightly pressed in center, and a cake tester comes out clean, 50 minutes to 1 hour. Transfer skillet to a wire rack to cool 20 minutes. Turn out cake onto a serving plate to cool completely before serving.

**BAKING TIP**

Instead of a
10-inch skillet, you
can use a 9-inch
round cake pan.

# Snickerdoodle Crumb Cake

**MAKES ONE 8-INCH SQUARE CAKE**

*True to the snickerdoodle spirit, cinnamon-sugar supplies
sweet crunch to this breakfast, snack, or anytime streusel-topped
crumb cake. Made from pantry staples, this is a treat you
can easily put together whenever the snickerdoodle craving strikes.*

---

**FOR THE STREUSEL**

½ cup unbleached
all-purpose flour

½ cup packed
light-brown sugar

½ teaspoon kosher salt

4 tablespoons cold unsalted
butter, cut into pieces

**FOR THE CAKE**

1½ sticks (¾ cup) unsalted
butter, melted and cooled,
plus more for pan

1½ cups unbleached
all-purpose flour

¼ teaspoon baking soda

½ teaspoon cream of tartar

½ teaspoon kosher salt

½ cup packed
light-brown sugar

½ cup plus 2 tablespoons
granulated sugar

3 large eggs,
room temperature

1 teaspoon ground
cinnamon

**1. Make the streusel:** In a small bowl, whisk together flour, brown sugar, and salt. Using your hands or a pastry cutter, cut in butter until small to medium clumps form. Refrigerate until ready to use.

**2. Make the cake:** Preheat oven to 350°F. Butter an 8-inch square baking pan. Line with parchment, leaving a 2-inch overhang on two sides; butter parchment. In a medium bowl, whisk together flour, baking soda, cream of tartar, and salt.

**3.** In a large bowl, whisk together butter, brown sugar, ½ cup granulated sugar, and the eggs. Add flour mixture and stir to combine. Spread half of batter in bottom of prepared pan. In a small bowl, stir together cinnamon and remaining 2 tablespoons granulated sugar; sprinkle half the mixture over the batter. Dollop remaining batter on top; spread evenly with an offset spatula or the back of a spoon. Sprinkle evenly with streusel, then remaining cinnamon-sugar.

**4.** Bake until top is browned and a cake tester comes out clean, 30 to 35 minutes. Transfer pan to a wire rack to cool completely. Using parchment overhang, remove cake from pan to a cutting board, and cut to serve. (Store in an airtight container at room temperature up to 3 days.)

# No-Bake Key Lime Cheesecake

SERVES 10 TO 12

*Deeply aromatic and flavorful, Key lime juice and zest give frothy mousse-like cheesecake the gently tart treatment. If you can't find Key limes, however, regular limes will do. With a crust that sets in the freezer, this no-oven-required cake is a summer go-to dessert.*

1 cup finely ground graham crackers (from 9 crackers)

3 tablespoons sugar

½ teaspoon kosher salt

5 tablespoons unsalted butter, melted and cooled

2 packages (8 ounces each) cream cheese, room temperature

1 can (14 ounces) sweetened condensed milk

2 teaspoons grated Key lime zest

⅓ cup fresh Key lime juice (from 16 limes)

½ teaspoon vanilla extract

½ cup cold heavy cream

Thinly sliced Key lime rounds, for serving

**1.** In a medium bowl, whisk together graham cracker crumbs, sugar, and salt. Stir in butter until mixture resembles wet sand and holds together when squeezed. Press evenly into the bottom of a 9-inch springform pan. Freeze until firm, about 15 minutes.

**2.** Meanwhile, with an electric mixer, beat cream cheese and condensed milk on medium-high speed until fluffy, about 5 minutes. Add lime zest, juice, and vanilla; beat 1 minute more.

**3.** In a separate bowl, whip cream to stiff peaks. Gently fold into cream cheese mixture. Pour over chilled crust; smooth top with an offset spatula. Cover with plastic and refrigerate at least 12 hours and up to 3 days.

**4.** Run a knife along cake's edge before releasing sides of pan, then under bottom to loosen. Serve, garnished with lime rounds.

**BAKING TIP**
Use the
bottom of a
measuring
cup to press
the crust into
the dish.

# PB&J Cheesecake

## MAKES TWENTY-FOUR 2-INCH SQUARES

*A classic sandwich combo gets elevated to a salty-sweet cake.
Peanuts make an already textured graham cracker crust pop and contrast
with an ultrasmooth peanut butter–cream cheese filling.
We topped it with Concord grape jelly, but choose your favorite.*

6 tablespoons unsalted butter, melted, plus more for brushing

14 graham cracker sheets (each 3 by 5 inches), broken into pieces

⅔ cup unsalted roasted peanuts

⅓ cup packed light-brown sugar

1 teaspoon kosher salt

4 packages (8 ounces each) cream cheese, room temperature

1 cup creamy peanut butter

1 cup granulated sugar

4 large eggs, room temperature

1 teaspoon vanilla extract

1 cup Concord grape jelly

**1.** Preheat oven to 350°F. Brush a 9-by-13-inch baking dish with butter.

**2.** Finely grind graham crackers in a food processor. Add melted butter, peanuts, brown sugar, and ½ teaspoon salt; pulse until peanuts are chopped and mixture resembles wet sand. Transfer to prepared baking dish; press firmly and evenly into bottom and three-quarters up sides. Bake until set and slightly darkened, 12 to 15 minutes. Transfer dish to a wire rack to cool completely.

**3.** Reduce oven to 325°F. With an electric mixer, beat cream cheese and peanut butter on medium speed until smooth. Gradually beat in granulated sugar until light and fluffy, scraping down sides of bowl as needed. Beat in remaining ½ teaspoon salt. Add eggs, one at a time, beating well after each addition; then stir in vanilla until smooth. Pour filling into cooked crust; smooth top with a small offset spatula. Bake until puffed and set along edges but still slightly wobbly in center, 40 to 45 minutes. Transfer dish to a wire rack to cool completely.

**4.** In a saucepan over medium heat, whisk jelly until melted. Pour evenly over cake, then tilt dish to spread jelly to edges in a thin, even layer. Refrigerate until jelly is firmly set, at least 4 hours and up to 3 days. To serve, cut cake into squares, wiping knife between cuts for clean edges.

# 4

# Sheet Cakes

*Perfectly portable, easy to slice and serve, and unfailingly delicious. Look to these single-layer stunners whenever you have a hungry crowd to feed or a party on the move.*

# Flourless Chocolate-Almond Sheet Cake

SERVES 12 TO 16

*Chocolate cake goes gluten-free simply by substituting almond flour
for all-purpose wheat. The bonus is deliciously nutty flavor and a decadent crumb.
The cake's surface might crack during baking, but don't
worry—a chocolate crème fraîche frosting will hide any imperfections.*

## FOR THE CAKE

1½ sticks (¾ cup) unsalted butter, room temperature, plus more for pan

1½ cups granulated sugar

9 large eggs, separated, room temperature

9 ounces bittersweet chocolate (70% cacao), melted and slightly cooled

1 tablespoon vanilla extract

2¼ cups almond flour or finely ground raw, whole almonds

1¼ teaspoons kosher salt

Chopped almonds, for serving (optional)

## FOR THE FROSTING

12 ounces cream cheese, room temperature

1½ sticks (¾ cup) unsalted butter, room temperature

4½ cups confectioners' sugar, sifted

½ cup unsweetened Dutch-process cocoa powder

¼ teaspoon kosher salt

1 pound 2 ounces bittersweet chocolate (70% cacao), melted and slightly cooled

1½ cups crème fraîche or sour cream

**1. Make the cake:** Preheat oven to 350°F. Butter a 9-by-13-inch baking pan. In a large bowl, with an electric mixer, beat butter with 1 cup granulated sugar on medium-high until pale and fluffy, 2 to 3 minutes. Beat in egg yolks, one at a time, beating well after each addition. Beat in chocolate and vanilla. Add almond flour and salt; beat to combine.

**2.** In a large bowl and using the whisk attachment, whisk egg whites on low speed until frothy. Increase speed to medium-high and whip to soft peaks, about 1 minute. Gradually add remaining ½ cup granulated sugar, beating until stiff, glossy peaks form, about 1 minute more. Stir one-third of egg-white mixture into batter until no streaks remain. Using a rubber spatula, gently fold in remaining egg-white mixture just to combine (do not overmix).

**3.** Transfer batter to prepared pan, smoothing top with an offset spatula. Bake, rotating pan halfway through, until set along edges but still slightly wobbly in center, 35 to 40 minutes. Transfer pan to a wire rack to cool completely.

**4. Make the frosting:** In a large bowl, beat cream cheese and butter with an electric mixer on medium speed until pale and fluffy, about 3 minutes. In a medium bowl, sift together confectioners' sugar, cocoa, and salt; gradually beat into cream cheese mixture. Continue beating while pouring melted chocolate in a slow, steady stream. Beat in crème fraîche until well combined. (If frosting isn't firm enough, refrigerate for 10 minutes, and beat before using.)

**5.** Spread frosting evenly over top of cake with an offset spatula. Sprinkle nuts, if using, over half of cake. Slice cake into squares. Serve immediately. (Store cake in refrigerator, wrapped in plastic, up to 3 days; return to room temperature before serving.)

**SERVING TIP**

To serve, try
spreading chopped
nuts over half the
cake, then slicing it
into squares and
arranging them in
an alternating
pattern, as shown.

# Chocolate Cake with Swiss Meringue Buttercream

### SERVES 12 TO 16

*This crowd-pleasing party cake feels subtly sophisticated, thanks to a rich dark chocolate flavor and chocolate curls instead of sprinkles on top. To make the curls, melt a semisweet chocolate bar in the microwave for just a few seconds to soften, then use a vegetable peeler to shave them right over the cake.*

1½ sticks (¾ cup) unsalted butter, room temperature, plus more for pan

½ cup boiling water

⅓ cup natural cocoa powder

3 ounces semisweet chocolate, finely chopped (½ cup)

2 cups unbleached all-purpose flour

1 teaspoon baking powder

½ teaspoon baking soda

1 teaspoon kosher salt

1½ cups sugar

2 large eggs, room temperature

2 teaspoons vanilla extract

1 cup sour cream

3 cups Swiss Meringue Buttercream (page 237)

Chocolate curls, for serving

**1.** Preheat oven to 350°F. Butter a 9-by-13-inch baking pan. Line with parchment; butter parchment. In a medium bowl, stir together boiling water, cocoa, and chocolate; let cool 10 minutes. Meanwhile, in a separate medium bowl, whisk together flour, baking powder, baking soda, and salt.

**2.** In a large bowl, with an electric mixer, beat butter with sugar on medium-high speed until fluffy, 2 to 3 minutes. Add eggs, one at a time, beating well after each addition and scraping down sides of bowl as needed. Beat in vanilla, then chocolate mixture. Reduce speed to low; beat in flour mixture in two batches, alternating with sour cream, until just combined. Transfer batter to prepared pan, smoothing top with an offset spatula.

**3.** Bake until a cake tester comes out with just a few moist crumbs, 35 to 40 minutes (top will not spring back). Transfer pan to a wire rack to cool 10 minutes. Invert onto a wire rack and remove parchment; let cool completely. (Cake can be made up to 1 day ahead and stored at room temperature, wrapped in plastic.)

**4.** Spread buttercream evenly over top and sides of cake with an offset spatula. Sprinkle with chocolate curls. (Store cake in refrigerator, wrapped in plastic, up to 3 days; return to room temperature before serving.)

# Strawberry Biscuit Sheet Cake

### SERVES 12

*The base of this dessert is as clever as it is divine: Individual biscuits are baked together into one rectangular sheet for a pretty presentation that easily breaks apart for serving. Top with the fruit of your choice; we went old-school with sweet strawberries but can't wait to try peaches and nectarines.*

**FOR THE BISCUIT SHEET CAKE**

4 cups cake flour (not self-rising), plus more for dusting

⅔ cup granulated sugar

5 teaspoons baking powder

2 teaspoons kosher salt

1½ sticks (¾ cup) cold unsalted butter, cut into pieces

1¼ cups buttermilk

Heavy cream, for brushing

Fine sanding sugar, for sprinkling (optional)

**FOR THE BERRIES AND CREAM**

4 cups sliced strawberries (from 2 quart containers)

5 tablespoons granulated sugar

¼ teaspoon kosher salt

2 teaspoons fresh lemon juice

1¼ cups heavy cream

1 vanilla bean, split and seeds scraped

3 tablespoons confectioners' sugar, sifted

Freeze-dried strawberries, finely ground, for serving (optional)

**1. Make the cake:** Preheat oven to 450°F. In a medium bowl, combine flour, granulated sugar, baking powder, and salt. Using a pastry cutter or your fingers, cut in butter until mixture resembles coarse meal. Add buttermilk and stir until just combined.

**2.** Turn out dough onto a lightly floured surface, kneading once or twice to help it come together. Pat into a 10-by-7-inch rectangle about ¾ inch thick. Cut lengthwise into thirds, then crosswise into fourths to create 12 equal pieces. Using a spatula, transfer to a 9½-by-12½-inch rimmed baking sheet or other pan, arranging pieces to roughly re-create original rectangle but leaving ½ inch between them.

**3.** Brush tops with cream and sprinkle generously with sanding sugar, if using. Bake, rotating sheet halfway through, until golden brown and cooked through, 25 to 28 minutes (gaps should be gone, so you have a single but easily separable biscuit). Transfer sheet to a wire rack to cool 10 minutes. Using two large spatulas, carefully lift whole biscuit onto rack to cool almost but not quite completely, about 1 hour.

**4. Make the berries and cream:** In a medium bowl, combine strawberries, granulated sugar, salt, and lemon juice; let stand, stirring occasionally, until juicy, about 30 minutes. With an electric mixer on medium-high speed, beat cream with vanilla seeds and confectioners' sugar until stiff peaks form.

**5.** Carefully slide whole biscuit onto a serving platter. Spoon 2 cups whipped cream over biscuit; top with 3 cups berry mixture, drizzling with some juices. Sprinkle with berry powder, if using; serve immediately, with remaining whipped cream and berries on the side.

# Cuatro Leches Cake

**SERVES 12 TO 16**

*We see your three-milk cake, and we raise you one more. This light, airy sponge cake gets soaked in the traditional trio of whole milk, condensed milk, and evaporated milk after baking—but we've also snuck milk powder into the batter to maximize tenderness. Make the dessert a day before serving so it can soak up all that goodness.*

Unsalted butter, for pan

1¼ cups cake flour
(not self-rising)

¼ cup nonfat milk powder

1 cup sugar

2 teaspoons baking powder

½ teaspoon kosher salt

1½ cups whole milk

⅓ cup safflower oil

5 large egg yolks
plus 6 large egg whites

1 vanilla bean, split and
seeds scraped

¼ teaspoon cream of tartar

1 can (14 ounces)
sweetened condensed milk

1 can (12 ounces)
evaporated milk

Whipped Cream
(page 242)

Sliced fruit, such as
mangoes and pineapple,
for serving

**1.** Preheat oven to 325°F. Butter a 9-by-13-inch baking pan. In a medium bowl, whisk together flour, milk powder, ½ cup sugar, the baking powder, and salt. In a separate medium bowl, whisk together ½ cup whole milk, the oil, egg yolks, and vanilla seeds. Whisk egg-yolk mixture into flour mixture until just combined.

**2.** With an electric mixer, whisk egg whites on high speed until frothy. Add cream of tartar and beat until soft peaks form, about 2 minutes. Gradually add remaining ½ cup sugar, beating until stiff, glossy peaks form, about 5 minutes. Using a rubber spatula, fold one-third of egg-white mixture into batter. Gently but thoroughly fold in remaining egg-white mixture. Transfer batter to prepared pan, smoothing top with an offset spatula. Bake, rotating pan halfway through, until top springs back when lightly touched, about 40 minutes.

**3.** In a medium bowl, whisk together condensed milk, evaporated milk, and remaining 1 cup whole milk. Poke warm cake all over with a wooden skewer or toothpick, then pour milk mixture over top. Let cool to room temperature, about 1 hour. Cover and refrigerate at least 2 hours and up to 2 days. Serve cake with whipped cream and sliced fruit.

# Ombré Sheet Cake

## SERVES 12 TO 16

*This artfully frosted vanilla cake, with its soft-pastel streaks of buttercream blending together like a painted sunset, might just elicit some oohs and aahs from your guests. The colors are all-natural, so you can feel good about them: Plant-based food dyes in yellow and pink provide the pleasing tints.*

1 stick (½ cup) plus 1 tablespoon unsalted butter, room temperature, plus more for pan

2¼ cups unbleached all–purpose flour, plus more for pan

1½ teaspoons baking powder

½ teaspoon baking soda

¾ teaspoon kosher salt

1 cup sugar

3 large eggs, room temperature

1 teaspoon vanilla extract

1 cup buttermilk, room temperature

Vanilla Buttercream (page 239)

Natural food dyes in Berry and Sunflower

**1.** Preheat oven to 350°F. Butter a 9-by-13-inch baking pan. Dust with flour, tapping out any excess. In a medium bowl, whisk together flour, baking powder, baking soda, and salt.

**2.** With an electric mixer, beat butter with sugar on medium speed until light and fluffy, about 5 minutes. Add eggs, one at a time, beating well after each addition and scraping down sides of bowl as needed. Beat in vanilla. Reduce speed to low and add flour mixture in two batches, alternating with buttermilk and beginning and ending with flour.

**3.** Transfer batter to prepared pan, smoothing top with an offset spatula. Bake, rotating pan halfway through, until cake is golden and puffed and a cake tester comes out clean, 22 to 25 minutes. Transfer pan to a wire rack to cool 30 minutes. Turn out onto a wire rack to cool completely.

**4.** Spread 2½ cups buttercream over top of cake with an offset spatula. Divide remaining buttercream among 4 small bowls (about ⅓ cup each). Use food dyes to create shades of yellow, peach, and two shades of pink. Let stand 10 minutes to allow dyes to fully saturate.

**5.** Transfer frostings into pastry bags (no tip required) and pipe a line of each color horizontally across top of cake in the desired order (we chose light to dark to mimic a sunset). Lightly drag a large offset spatula or bench scraper end to end across cake to create a blended effect. Add more frosting as desired. Be sure to wipe off the spatula or bench scraper completely between strokes. (Alternatively, for a more abstract design, instead of piping the colored frosting, you can use a small offset spatula and randomly scatter a few dollops of colored frosting around the cake, then blend as directed. More white space will create a lighter effect; closer together will be more pigmented.)

# Vanilla Sheet Cake with Citrus Cream Cheese Frosting

SERVES 12 TO 16

*Be the hero of the spring bake sale, picnic, or dinner party when you walk in with this treat. It's super simple, which is part of what makes it so lovely: tender vanilla cake with a generous citrusy cream cheese frosting. We used slices of lemons and limes to garnish, but this could also be a gorgeous platform for fresh berries.*

1 stick (½ cup) plus 1 tablespoon unsalted butter, room temperature, plus more for pan

2¼ cups unbleached all-purpose flour, plus more for pan

1½ teaspoons baking powder

½ teaspoon baking soda

¾ teaspoon kosher salt

1 cup sugar

3 large eggs, room temperature

1 teaspoon vanilla extract

¼ teaspoon finely grated lemon zest

1 cup buttermilk, room temperature

Citrus Cream Cheese Frosting (page 240)

Citrus slices, quartered, for serving (optional)

**1.** Preheat oven to 350°F. Lightly butter a 9-by-13-inch baking pan. Dust with flour, tapping out any excess. In a medium bowl, whisk together flour, baking powder, baking soda, and salt.

**2.** In a separate medium bowl, beat butter and sugar with an electric mixer on medium speed until light and fluffy, about 5 minutes. Add eggs, one at a time, beating well after each addition and scraping down sides of bowl as needed. Beat in vanilla and lemon zest. Reduce speed to low and add flour mixture in two batches, alternating with buttermilk and beginning and ending with flour, scraping down sides of bowl as needed.

**3.** Transfer batter to prepared pan, smoothing top with an offset spatula. Bake, rotating pan halfway through, until cake is golden and puffed and a cake tester comes out clean, 22 to 25 minutes. Transfer pan to a wire rack to cool completely.

**4.** Spread frosting evenly over top of cake with an offset spatula. Slice cake, garnish with lemon and lime slices, if desired, and serve.

# Chocolate Zucchini Cake

### SERVES 10 TO 12

*The ubiquitous vegetable brings subtle flavor and incredible moisture
to this cake—so you can bake it ahead—while two types of chocolate and tangy
cream cheese frosting are the stars of the show. As a pretty hint
at your secret ingredient, candy some zucchini blossoms to scatter on top.*

---

## FOR THE CAKE

1 stick (½ cup) unsalted butter,
melted, plus more for pan

1¾ cups unbleached
all-purpose flour

½ cup unsweetened Dutch-
process cocoa powder

1¾ cups sugar

1½ teaspoons baking powder

¼ teaspoon baking soda

1 teaspoon kosher salt

4 large eggs,
room temperature

2 teaspoons vanilla extract

4 cups grated zucchini (from
2 medium), drained and
squeezed of excess moisture

5 ounces semisweet
chocolate, chopped (1 cup)

Cream Cheese
Frosting (page 240)

## FOR THE CANDIED
## ZUCCHINI BLOSSOMS

2 ounces zucchini
blossoms (about 8)

½ teaspoon safflower oil

1 tablespoon sugar

**1. Make the cake:** Preheat oven to 350°F. Butter a 10-by-15-inch jelly-roll pan. Line bottom with parchment, leaving a 2-inch overhang on two sides; butter parchment.

**2.** In a large bowl, whisk together flour, cocoa, sugar, baking powder, baking soda, and salt. In a medium bowl, whisk together eggs, butter, and vanilla. Stir egg mixture into flour mixture until just combined, about 1 minute. Stir in zucchini and chocolate (batter will be quite thick). Transfer batter to prepared pan, smoothing top with an offset spatula. Bake, rotating pan halfway through, until a cake tester comes out clean, 28 to 30 minutes. Transfer pan to a wire rack to cool. Using parchment overhang, turn out cake onto rack to cool completely.

**3. Make the candied zucchini blossoms:** Reduce oven to 275°F. Line a rimmed baking sheet with a nonstick baking mat or parchment. Halve blossoms lengthwise and remove stamens. In a medium bowl, very gently toss with oil and sugar, place on prepared sheet, and bake 10 minutes. Using an offset spatula, gently flip blossoms; bake 5 minutes more, then flip again. Repeat, checking frequently to avoid burning, until dry to the touch, about 20 minutes more. Transfer sheet to a wire rack to cool completely. (Blossoms can be stored in an airtight container in a cool, dry place up to 3 days. Recrisp in a 275°F oven before using.)

**4.** Spread frosting evenly over top of cake with an offset spatula. Garnish with zucchini blossoms and serve. (Cake can be refrigerated, without blossoms, up to 8 hours.)

# Semolina Coconut Cake

SERVES 12

*With its pleasantly coarse crumb and golden hue, you might expect this Middle Eastern–inspired cake to be made from cornmeal, but it's actually semolina, the same hearty wheat flour often used in pasta. Coconut and pistachios lend delightful texture and flavor to the simple, not-too-sweet cake.*

**FOR THE SYRUP**

2 cups sugar

Pinch of saffron threads

2 tablespoons fresh lemon juice

**FOR THE CAKE**

Unsalted butter, for pan

Pinch of saffron threads

1¼ cups whole milk, warmed

2 cups desiccated coconut (unsweetened, dried, and shredded)

1½ cups semolina flour

1½ teaspoons baking powder

½ teaspoon kosher salt

2 large eggs, room temperature

½ cup sugar

½ cup safflower oil

1 cup plain whole-milk yogurt

¼ cup pistachios, finely chopped

**1. Make the syrup:** In a small saucepan, combine sugar, saffron, lemon juice, and ½ cup water. Bring to a boil, reduce to a simmer, and stir constantly until sugar is dissolved, about 2 minutes.

**2. Make the cake:** Preheat oven to 350°F. Butter a 9-by-13-inch baking pan and line with parchment, leaving a 2-inch overhang on all sides.

**3.** In a small bowl, add saffron to milk and let steep 5 minutes. In a large bowl, whisk together coconut, semolina flour, baking powder, and salt until combined. In a separate large bowl, whisk together eggs, sugar, and oil until light and fluffy. Add milk mixture and yogurt; stir to combine. Fold in coconut mixture to incorporate.

**4.** Transfer batter to prepared pan, smoothing top with an offset spatula. Bake, rotating pan halfway through, until cake is golden brown and springs back in center when gently touched, about 1 hour.

**5.** Transfer pan to a wire rack. Pour syrup over warm cake and sprinkle with pistachios. Let cake cool completely in pan on rack. Using parchment overhang, remove cake from pan to a cutting board. Cut into triangles using a serrated knife and serve.

# Confetti Cake with Vanilla Frosting

### SERVES 16

*Homemade sprinkles for this festive cake take this kid's party standby to a whole new level. They're not only surprisingly easy to master, but they taste good—which makes a big difference when you're stirring one-third of a cup into your batter. Plus, you can break some into long pieces for garnish and let their soft, beautiful colors charm the table.*

---

## FOR THE CAKE

2 sticks (1 cup) unsalted butter, room temperature, cut into tablespoons, plus more for pan

3 cups unbleached all-purpose flour, plus more for pan

1¼ cups whole milk

4 large eggs, room temperature

2 teaspoons vanilla extract

1¾ cups sugar

1 tablespoon baking powder

1 teaspoon kosher salt

⅓ cup packed Homemade Sprinkles (page 244), plus additional larger pieces for garnish

## FOR THE FROSTING

¼ cup unbleached all-purpose flour

1 cup whole milk

1 teaspoon vanilla extract

Pinch of kosher salt

2 sticks (1 cup) unsalted butter, room temperature

1 cup sugar

**1. Make the cake:** Preheat oven to 350°F. Butter a 9-by-13-inch baking pan. Line pan with parchment, leaving a 2-inch overhang on long sides; butter parchment. Dust with flour, tapping out any excess. In a medium bowl, whisk together milk, eggs, and vanilla.

**2.** With an electric mixer, beat flour, sugar, baking powder, and salt on low speed until well combined, about 1 minute. Continue beating while gradually adding butter until mixture is crumbly, about 3 minutes. Slowly add half of milk mixture; increase speed to medium and beat until fluffy, about 1 minute. Slowly add remaining half of milk mixture, scraping down sides of bowl as needed. Beat until incorporated, about 30 seconds more.

**3.** Fold in sprinkles with a spatula. Pour batter into prepared pan; tap on counter. Bake, rotating pan halfway through, until golden brown and a cake tester comes out clean, 30 to 35 minutes. Transfer pan to a wire rack to cool completely. Using parchment overhang, remove cake from pan to a cake plate.

**4. Make the frosting:** In a small saucepan, whisk together flour and milk until smooth. Cook over medium-high heat, whisking constantly, until mixture becomes thick and resembles pudding, 3 to 4 minutes. Transfer to a heatproof bowl; stir in vanilla and salt. Press plastic wrap directly on surface and let cool completely.

**5.** In a medium bowl, with an electric mixer on medium speed, beat butter and sugar until light and fluffy, scraping down sides of bowl as needed, about 2 minutes. Add milk mixture and continue beating until frosting is light and fluffy and resembles whipped cream, about 2 minutes more. Spread frosting evenly over top of cake with an offset spatula, and top with large sprinkles. (Store cake in refrigerator, wrapped in plastic, up to 3 days; return to room temperature before serving.)

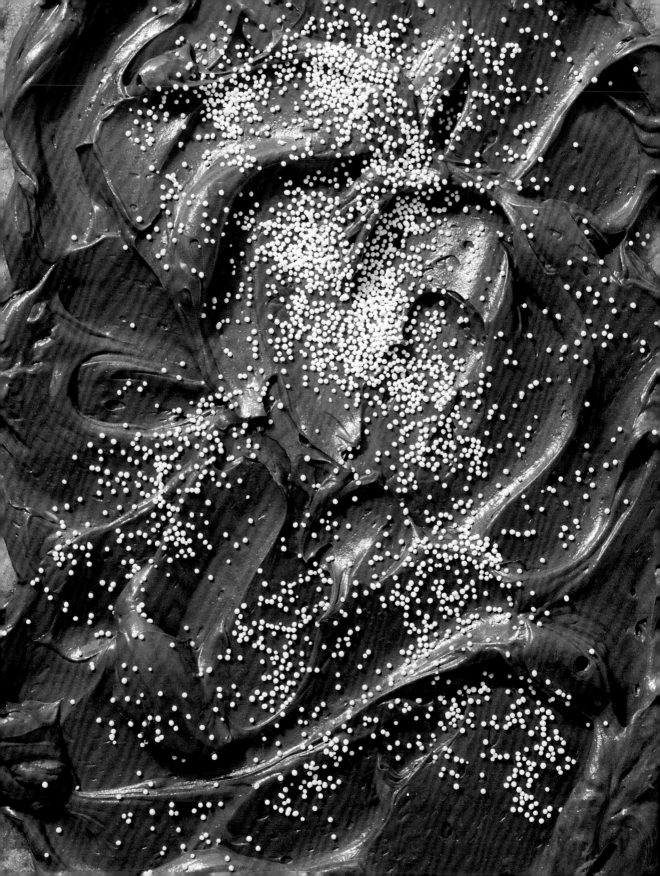

# Vanilla Cake with Chocolate Ganache Buttercream

**SERVES 16 TO 20**

*No plain vanilla here: This ultra-moist cake features layers of flavor—with vanilla extract as well as seeds scraped right from the pod (or try substituting 2 teaspoons vanilla paste)—and a luscious topping of chocolate ganache buttercream. It's a birthday classic, only better.*

---

## FOR THE CAKE

1½ sticks (¾ cup) unsalted butter, room temperature, plus more for pan

1½ cups sugar

2¼ teaspoons baking powder

1½ teaspoons kosher salt

1 large egg plus 4 large yolks, room temperature

1 vanilla bean, split and seeds scraped

1 teaspoon vanilla extract

2¼ cups unbleached all-purpose flour

¾ cup whole milk, room temperature

White nonpareils, for garnish

## FOR THE CHOCOLATE GANACHE BUTTERCREAM

8 ounces semisweet chocolate, finely chopped (1¾ cups)

¾ cup heavy cream

1 tablespoon light corn syrup

1½ sticks (¾ cup) unsalted butter, cut into pieces, room temperature

**1. Make the cake:** Preheat oven to 350°F. Butter a 9-by-13-inch baking pan. With an electric mixer, beat butter with sugar, baking powder, and salt on medium speed until light and fluffy, about 3 minutes. Add egg and yolks, one at a time, beating well after each addition and scraping down sides of bowl as needed. Beat in both vanillas, then flour in three additions, alternating with milk and beginning and ending with flour. Transfer batter to prepared pan, smoothing top with an offset spatula.

**2.** Bake until a cake tester comes out with a few moist crumbs, 35 to 40 minutes. Transfer pan to a wire rack to cool completely.

**3. Make the buttercream:** Place chocolate in large heatproof bowl. In a small saucepan, bring cream and corn syrup to a boil. Pour mixture over chocolate; let stand 2 minutes, then stir until smooth. Let cool 30 minutes. With an electric mixer on medium-high speed, beat, gradually adding butter, until all has been added and buttercream is silky and smooth. Continue beating, scraping down sides of bowl as needed, until light and fluffy, about 1 minute more.

**4.** Spread buttercream evenly over top of cake with an offset spatula. Sprinkle with white nonpareils. (Store cake in refrigerator, wrapped in plastic, up to 3 days; return to room temperature before serving.)

# Lemon-Glazed Sheet Cake

**SERVES 12 TO 16**

*We couldn't get enough of this pleasantly tart sheet cake and its double dose of tangy brightness, thanks to a zest-filled batter and a silky citrus glaze. Left plain, the glaze gives each square a sweet modern look, but you could also dot the cake with candied lemon zest for a little more wow.*

---

## FOR THE CAKE

1 stick (½ cup) plus
2 tablespoons unsalted
butter, room temperature,
plus more for pan

1⅓ cups sugar

1½ teaspoons baking powder

¼ teaspoon baking soda

1¼ teaspoons kosher salt

2 teaspoons grated lemon zest
plus 1 tablespoon fresh juice

2 large eggs,
room temperature

1⅔ cups cake flour
(not self-rising)

½ cup whole milk,
room temperature

## FOR THE GLAZE

¾ cup sugar

¼ cup cornstarch

½ teaspoon kosher salt

1½ teaspoons grated lemon
zest plus ⅔ cup fresh juice
(from about 3 lemons)

4 large egg yolks,
room temperature

4 tablespoons unsalted butter,
room temperature

**1. Make the cake:** Preheat oven to 350°F. Butter a 9-by-13-inch baking pan. With an electric mixer on medium-high speed, beat butter with sugar, baking powder, baking soda, salt, and lemon zest until light and fluffy, about 3 minutes. Add eggs, one at a time, beating well after each addition and scraping down sides of bowl as needed. Beat in lemon juice. Beat in flour in three additions, alternating with milk and beginning and ending with flour. Transfer batter to prepared pan, smoothing top with an offset spatula.

**2.** Bake until a cake tester comes out with a few moist crumbs, 30 to 35 minutes. Transfer pan to a wire rack to cool completely.

**3. Make the glaze:** In a medium saucepan, combine sugar, cornstarch, salt, and lemon zest. Whisk in yolks, then 1⅔ cups water, the lemon juice, and butter. Bring to a boil over medium-high heat, whisking constantly, and cook, still whisking, until slightly thickened, about 1 minute. Strain through a fine-mesh sieve into a heatproof bowl. Let stand 30 minutes, whisking occasionally.

**4.** Poke 20 holes in cake with a skewer; pour glaze over top. Refrigerate at least 2 hours and up to overnight. (Store cake in refrigerator, wrapped in plastic, up to 3 days; return to room temperature before serving.)

# No-Bake Banana Split Sheet Cake

**SERVES 12**

*This crowd-size play on everyone's favorite sundae features vanilla semifreddo—an Italian frozen custard made with cream, sugar, egg yolks, and gelatin—that is layered between banana slices and store-bought chocolate wafers. Of course, it wouldn't be a banana split without a drizzle of caramel, whipped cream, a sprinkle of nuts, and a cherry or two.*

---

2 tablespoons vanilla extract

2 tablespoons cold water

2¼ teaspoons unflavored gelatin (1 envelope)

4 large eggs, separated, room temperature

1 cup granulated sugar

3½ cups heavy cream

1 vanilla bean, split and seeds scraped

1 box (9 ounces) chocolate-wafer cookies, such as Nabisco Famous Wafers (42 total)

3 to 4 bananas, peeled and sliced crosswise ¼ inch thick (about 2½ cups)

16 maraschino cherries, stemmed and halved, plus whole ones for serving

Caramel Sauce (page 242)

1 tablespoon confectioners' sugar

Chopped walnuts, for serving

**1.** In a small bowl, combine vanilla extract and cold water. Sprinkle with gelatin; let stand 5 minutes. In a heatproof bowl set over (not in) a pot of simmering water, combine egg yolks and ½ cup granulated sugar. Whisk until pale and thickened, about 2 minutes. Whisk in gelatin mixture until dissolved. Transfer mixture to a cool bowl.

**2.** In a large bowl, with an electric mixer on medium-high speed, beat 2½ cups heavy cream with the vanilla seeds until stiff peaks form. Fold one-third of whipped cream into gelatin mixture, then fold gelatin mixture into remaining whipped cream.

**3.** In a large bowl, beat egg whites with electric mixer on medium-high speed until soft peaks form, about 2 minutes. Gradually add remaining ½ cup granulated sugar and beat to stiff peaks, 5 to 6 minutes. Fold into cream mixture. (You should have about 9 cups total.)

**4.** Line a 9-by-13-inch baking pan with plastic wrap, leaving a 4-inch overhang on all sides. Arrange 18 cookies on bottom of pan, slightly overlapping. Arrange bananas in a single layer over cookies. Spread 4 cups cream mixture evenly on top. Arrange 12 more cookies on top of cream. Fold halved cherries into remaining cream mixture, then spread evenly over cookies. Arrange remaining 12 cookies on top. Wrap in plastic and freeze at least 4 hours and up to 3 days.

**5.** Remove pan from freezer; using plastic overhang, remove and invert cake onto a platter (if it's sticking, rub sides and bottom of pan with a warm, moist kitchen towel to loosen). Remove plastic and trim cake edges. Drizzle with ½ cup caramel. With an electric mixer on medium-high speed, beat remaining 1 cup heavy cream with the confectioners' sugar to stiff peaks; dollop over cake. Sprinkle with chopped walnuts and whole cherries; serve immediately with remaining caramel on the side.

# Spiced Snacking Cake

SERVES 12 TO 16

*Perfect for an after-school bite or a nibble with tea, snacking cake
is simple by design. This one is brimming with warm
spices and finished with a lemony glaze that's flecked with vanilla—
you can just drizzle it on with no frosting fussiness.*

## FOR THE CAKE

¼ cup plus 2 tablespoons
safflower oil, plus more for pan

2¼ cups unbleached
all-purpose flour

1½ cups granulated sugar

1 tablespoon plus
½ teaspoon baking powder

¾ teaspoon kosher salt

¾ teaspoon ground cinnamon

¼ teaspoon ground cardamom

1 large egg plus 1 large egg
yolk, room temperature

¾ cup sour cream

2¼ teaspoons vanilla extract

3 tablespoons whole milk

## FOR THE GLAZE

¾ cup confectioners' sugar

1½ tablespoons whole milk

1 vanilla bean, split and
seeds scraped

1½ teaspoons to 1 tablespoon
lemon zest, to taste

1 to 3 tablespoons freshly
squeezed lemon juice

**1. Make the cake:** Preheat oven to 350°F. Oil a 9-by-13-inch baking pan. Line with parchment, leaving an overhang on two sides; oil parchment. In a large bowl, whisk together flour, granulated sugar, baking powder, salt, cinnamon, and cardamom.

**2.** In a medium bowl, whisk together egg and egg yolk, sour cream, oil, vanilla, and milk until combined. Add egg mixture to flour mixture and stir until smooth (the batter will be thick). Transfer batter to prepared pan, smoothing top with an offset spatula. Bake until lightly golden and top of cake springs back when lightly pressed, 35 to 40 minutes. Transfer pan to a wire rack to cool 30 minutes. Using parchment overhang, remove cake from pan onto a rack to cool completely.

**3. Make the glaze:** In a small bowl, whisk together confectioners' sugar, milk, vanilla seeds, 1½ teaspoons lemon zest (add up to 1 tablespoon for a zesty bite), and 1 tablespoon lemon juice until smooth and pourable (if glaze is too thick, add up to remaining 2 tablespoons lemon juice). Pour over top of cake, spreading to edges with an offset spatula. Allow to set before slicing, about 30 minutes. (Store cake in refrigerator, wrapped in plastic, up to 3 days; return to room temperature before serving.)

# No-Bake Blueberry Ricotta Cheesecake

SERVES 14 TO 16

*This dessert is the perfect respite for those warm summer days—no oven required: Press a simple vanilla-wafer-crumb crust into a pan, and let it chill while you fold whipped cream into lemony ricotta and cream cheese for an airy filling. Blueberries—in both syrup form and fresh to maximize their in-season goodness—top the cool, cloudlike cake.*

---

1 box (11 ounces) vanilla-wafer cookies, such as Nabisco Nilla Wafers

¼ cup plus 3 tablespoons granulated sugar

½ teaspoon kosher salt

1 stick (½ cup) unsalted butter, melted

1 cup whole-milk ricotta

2 packages (8 ounces each) cream cheese, room temperature

1 cup confectioners' sugar, sifted

1 tablespoon finely grated lemon zest plus ¼ cup fresh juice (from 1 to 2 lemons)

1¼ cups heavy cream

5 cups blueberries (from 3 pint containers)

1½ teaspoons cornstarch

Fresh mint leaves, for serving

**1.** Pulse cookies in a food processor until finely ground. Add ¼ cup granulated sugar, ¼ teaspoon salt, and the butter; pulse until all crumbs are moist (you should have about 3½ cups). Press mixture into the bottom of a 9-by-13-inch baking pan; refrigerate while making filling.

**2.** Blend ricotta, cream cheese, confectioners' sugar, zest, and 3 tablespoons lemon juice in clean food processor until very smooth. Transfer to a large bowl. In a medium bowl, beat cream with an electric mixer on medium-high speed to stiff peaks, then fold into ricotta mixture.

**3.** Dollop 2½ cups cream mixture over crust; spread evenly to cover with an offset spatula. Top with 2 cups berries. Dollop with remaining cream mixture; spread to cover berries. Wrap in plastic and refrigerate at least 8 hours and up to 2 days.

**4.** In a small saucepan over medium-high heat, combine 1½ cups blueberries with 2 tablespoons water, remaining 3 tablespoons granulated sugar, 1 tablespoon lemon juice, and ¼ teaspoon salt. Cook, stirring, until blueberries begin to burst, 2 to 3 minutes. In a small bowl, whisk together cornstarch and 2 tablespoons water; stir into blueberry mixture. Bring to a boil, then cook 1 minute more, until slightly thickened. Remove from heat. Stir in 1 more cup berries; let cool completely. Spoon berry mixture over chilled cake. Garnish with remaining ½ cup berries and the mint leaves. (Store cake in refrigerator, wrapped in plastic, up to 2 days.)

# 5

# Cupcakes

*We remain steadfastly loyal to these miniature delights. Take the beloved standbys up a notch with sophisticated flavors (chocolate stout), surprising centers (orange curd), and pastry-chef-quality finishing touches (piped succulents).*

# Soft-Serve Peanut Butter Cupcakes

**MAKES 1 DOZEN**

*We'll still chase after the ice-cream truck for a soft-serve with a hard chocolate shell. These chocolate cupcakes with tall swirls of peanut butter and buttercream evoke all that nostalgic goodness. Hold each cupcake over the melted chocolate for a few seconds after dipping to catch extra drips.*

---

### FOR THE CUPCAKES

1½ cups sugar

1½ cups unbleached all–purpose flour

¾ cup unsweetened Dutch–process cocoa powder

1½ teaspoons baking soda

1 teaspoon baking powder

¾ teaspoon kosher salt

¾ cup buttermilk, room temperature

⅓ cup plus 1 tablespoon safflower oil

¾ cup warm water

2 large eggs, room temperature

1 teaspoon vanilla extract

### FOR THE BUTTERCREAM

Swiss Meringue Buttercream (page 237)

½ cup creamy peanut butter

¼ teaspoon kosher salt

1 teaspoon vanilla extract

### FOR THE GLAZE

12 ounces semisweet chocolate, coarsely chopped

3 tablespoons safflower oil

**1. Make the cupcakes:** Preheat oven to 350°F. Line a standard 12-cup muffin tin with paper liners. In a large bowl, whisk together sugar, flour, cocoa, baking soda, baking powder, and salt. Add buttermilk, oil, and warm water, and whisk to combine. Add eggs, one at a time, and then vanilla, whisking until smooth.

**2.** Divide batter evenly among prepared cups, filling each about two-thirds full. Bake, rotating tin halfway through, until cupcakes spring back to the touch and a cake tester comes out with a few moist crumbs attached, 20 to 25 minutes. Transfer tin to a wire rack to cool 10 minutes. Turn out cupcakes onto rack to cool completely.

**3. Make the buttercream:** Divide Swiss Meringue Buttercream in half. Stir peanut butter and salt into one half, and place into a pastry bag with no tip. Stir vanilla into other half, and place into another pastry bag with no tip. Fit a pastry bag with a large round tip, about ½ inch in diameter. Snip ends off both bags of buttercream and insert them into the pastry bag with the tip. Squeeze gently until both flavor buttercreams come out evenly. Pipe a swirl of buttercream onto each cupcake about 2 inches high. Chill cupcakes in refrigerator for at least 25 minutes.

**4. Make the glaze:** In a heatproof bowl set over (not in) a pan of simmering water, melt chocolate and oil, stirring until smooth. Remove from heat; let cool. Transfer to a tall, wide container, such as a quart takeout container, and let cool to room temperature. (The glaze should be smooth but not warm.) Gently dip cupcakes into glaze to coat tops completely, holding above container to allow excess glaze to drip off. Return cupcakes to refrigerator to set, about 10 minutes, before serving. (Cupcakes can be stored in the refrigerator up to 3 days.)

# Neapolitan Cupcakes

**MAKES 1 DOZEN**

*Vanilla, chocolate, and strawberry. With Neapolitan ice cream,
you don't have to choose. These cupcakes took that inspiration and ran
with it, layering chocolate and vanilla cake in each
cup and piling luscious strawberry buttercream on top.*

1¾ cups unbleached all-
purpose flour

2 teaspoons baking powder

1 teaspoon kosher salt

1 stick (½ cup) unsalted butter,
room temperature

1 cup sugar

3 large eggs,
room temperature

1 teaspoon vanilla extract

⅔ cup buttermilk,
room temperature

¼ cup unsweetened Dutch-
process cocoa powder

¼ cup hot water

2 ounces semisweet
chocolate (61% cacao),
coarsely chopped

Strawberry Buttercream
(page 239)

**1.** Preheat oven to 350°F. Line a standard 12-cup muffin tin with paper liners. In a medium bowl, whisk together flour, baking powder, and salt.

**2.** In a large bowl, with an electric mixer, beat butter and sugar on medium speed until light and fluffy, about 5 minutes. Add eggs, one at a time, beating well after each addition and scraping down sides of bowl as needed. Beat in vanilla. Reduce speed to low; add flour mixture in two batches, alternating with buttermilk and beginning and ending with flour.

**3.** In a small bowl, whisk together cocoa and hot water until smooth. Transfer 1 heaping cup vanilla batter to a medium bowl. Add cocoa mixture and stir until just combined; fold in chopped chocolate.

**4.** Divide chocolate batter evenly among prepared cups; top with remaining vanilla batter. Bake, rotating tin halfway through, until golden brown and a cake tester comes out clean, 20 to 22 minutes. Transfer tin to a wire rack to cool 10 minutes. Turn out cupcakes onto rack to cool completely. Just before serving, spread buttercream over cupcakes with an offset spatula. (Cupcakes can be stored up to 1 day in an airtight container at room temperature.)

# Blueberry Cupcakes

**MAKES 1 DOZEN**

*The blueberry muffin moves to prime time: Fresh, plump blueberries are mixed into vanilla cake—richer and sweeter than muffin batter—and then sprinkled with a crumbly cinnamon-sugar topping and swirls of blueberry-cream cheese icing.*

---

**FOR THE TOPPING**

6 tablespoons granulated sugar

¼ cup packed dark-brown sugar

1 teaspoon cinnamon

**FOR THE CUPCAKES**

1⅔ cups cake flour (not self-rising)

¼ teaspoon baking soda

1 teaspoon baking powder

½ teaspoon kosher salt

1 stick (½ cup) unsalted butter, room temperature

⅔ cup granulated sugar

2 large eggs, room temperature

1 teaspoon vanilla extract

¾ cup sour cream

6 ounces blueberries (1¼ cups)

**FOR THE ICING**

1 stick (½ cup) plus 2 tablespoons unsalted butter, room temperature

8 ounces cream cheese, room temperature

½ teaspoon vanilla extract

2⅔ cups confectioners' sugar

¼ cup blueberry jam, strained

**1. Make the topping:** In a small bowl, mix together both sugars and cinnamon.

**2. Make the cupcakes:** Preheat oven to 375°F with rack in upper third. Line a standard 12-cup muffin tin with paper liners. In a medium bowl, whisk together flour, baking soda, baking powder, and salt.

**3.** With an electric mixer on medium-high speed, beat together butter and granulated sugar in a large bowl until pale and fluffy, 2 to 3 minutes. Add eggs, one at a time, beating well after each addition and scraping down sides of bowl as needed. Beat in vanilla. Reduce speed to low and add flour mixture in three batches, alternating with sour cream and beginning and ending with flour. Fold in blueberries.

**4.** Divide batter evenly among prepared cups. Sprinkle topping, pressing to adhere to batter. Bake, rotating tin halfway through, until golden and a cake tester comes out with moist crumbs attached, 20 to 21 minutes. Transfer tin to a wire rack to cool 10 minutes. Turn out cupcakes onto rack to cool completely.

**5. Make the icing:** With an electric mixer on medium-high speed, beat together butter and cream cheese in a large bowl until pale and fluffy, about 2 minutes. Reduce speed to low, and gradually beat in vanilla and confectioners' sugar. Increase speed to medium-high and beat 1 minute. Spoon jam on top of icing and, without stirring, spoon icing into a pastry bag fitted with a ¾-inch tip. Pipe swirled mounds of icing on top of each cupcake. (Cupcakes can be refrigerated up to 6 hours; bring to room temperature 45 minutes before serving.)

# Molten Chocolate Espresso Cupcakes

**MAKES 6**

*When you have guests you want to impress but not much time, whip up a batch of these bittersweet, gooey, single-serving treats. Offer them a variety of ways— leave a couple plain, sprinkle others with flaky sea salt, top some with chopped pistachios—so everybody has their chocolate just the way they like it.*

---

4 tablespoons unsalted butter, room temperature, plus more for tin

⅓ cup sugar, plus more for tin

8 ounces bittersweet chocolate, coarsely chopped

⅓ cup unbleached all-purpose flour

1 tablespoon instant espresso powder

¼ teaspoon kosher salt

3 large eggs, room temperature

1 teaspoon vanilla extract

Chocolate Ganache Glaze (page 241)

Flaky sea salt, such as Maldon, and chopped pistachios, for sprinkling

**1.** Preheat oven to 400°F. Butter 6 cups of a standard muffin tin and dust with sugar; tap out any excess. In a heatproof bowl set over (not in) a pan of simmering water, melt chocolate, stirring until smooth. Remove from heat; let cool. In a medium bowl, whisk together flour, espresso powder, and salt.

**2.** With an electric mixer on medium-high speed, beat butter and sugar until light and fluffy. Add eggs, one at a time, beating well after each addition. Reduce speed to low. Add flour mixture and beat until combined. Beat in vanilla and melted chocolate.

**3.** Divide batter evenly among prepared cups. Bake, rotating tin halfway through, until cakes no longer jiggle when tin is shaken, 8 to 10 minutes. Transfer tin to a wire rack to cool 10 minutes. Turn out cakes onto rack to cool completely. (Store unglazed cakes, tightly covered, at room temperature for up to 5 days; glaze before serving.) Just before serving, spread ganache over tops with an offset spatula, and sprinkle with flaky salt and pistachios as desired.

# Orange Curd Cupcakes

MAKES 18

*These cupcakes get their citrusy zing from oranges in three ways: zest in the batter, curd in the filling, and dried, candied orange slices crowning the swirl of vanilla buttercream on top. Plan on making the orange curd and orange slices first, as they each need about 2 hours to set—or make them the day before.*

## FOR THE DRIED ORANGE SLICES

2 navel oranges, thinly sliced

½ cup confectioners' sugar, sifted

## FOR THE CUPCAKES

1¼ cups unbleached all-purpose flour

1¼ cups cake flour (not self-rising)

1¼ teaspoons baking powder

¼ teaspoon baking soda

¾ teaspoon kosher salt

1 stick (½ cup) unsalted butter, room temperature

1 cup granulated sugar

Grated zest of 1 orange

1 vanilla bean, split and seeds scraped

2 large eggs plus 2 large egg yolks, room temperature

1 cup buttermilk

Orange Curd (page 233)

Vanilla Buttercream (page 239)

**1. Make the dried orange slices:** Preheat oven to 200°F. Place orange slices in a single layer on a baking sheet lined with a nonstick baking mat. Generously dust oranges with confectioners' sugar. Bake until peels are dry and flesh is translucent, about 2½ hours.

**2. Make the cupcakes:** Increase oven to 350°F with rack in center. Line 2 standard 12-cup muffin tins with 18 paper liners. In a medium bowl, whisk together both flours, baking powder, baking soda, and salt.

**3.** In a large bowl, with an electric mixer on medium speed, beat butter and granulated sugar until fluffy, about 3 minutes. Beat in orange zest and vanilla seeds. Add whole eggs and yolks, one at a time, beating well after each addition. Reduce speed to low; gradually add flour mixture in three batches, alternating with buttermilk, beginning and ending with flour mixture, and beating until just combined.

**4.** Divide batter evenly among prepared cups, filling each two-thirds full. Bake, rotating tins halfway through, until cupcakes spring back when lightly pressed and a cake tester comes out clean, about 16 minutes. Transfer tins to a wire rack to cool 15 minutes. Turn out cupcakes to a serving platter to cool completely.

**5.** Fill a pastry bag fitted with a ¼-inch round tip with about 2 cups orange curd. Insert tip into center of each cupcake, squeezing gently to just fill. (Refrigerate unfrosted cakes in an airtight container for up to 3 days; frost before serving.) Fill another pastry bag fitted with a ½-inch star tip with buttercream and pipe onto cupcakes. Decorate with dried orange slices before serving. (Cupcakes can be refrigerated, in an airtight container, up to 3 days.)

**SERVING TIP**
Press the berries
gently into the
frosting, so they
don't roll away when
guests reach for
their cupcakes.

# Pull-Apart Vanilla Cupcakes with Berries

**MAKES 1 DOZEN**

*This dessert may look like a sheet cake on the top, but it's all cupcake on the bottom. For this fun twist, cupcakes are arranged in a snug rectangle with whipped-cream frosting blanketing them. Simply pull off servings—no slicing required.*

45 vanilla-wafer cookies (from one 11-ounce box), such as Nabisco Nilla Wafers, pulsed in a food processor until finely ground (about 1½ cups)

½ cup unbleached all-purpose flour

1 teaspoon baking powder

¼ teaspoon kosher salt

1 stick (½ cup) unsalted butter, room temperature

¾ cup granulated sugar

2 large eggs, room temperature

¾ cup whole milk

1 cup sweetened shredded coconut

1 teaspoon unflavored gelatin

1 cup cold heavy cream

2 tablespoons confectioners' sugar, sifted

¼ teaspoon vanilla extract

1½ cups mixed fresh berries, such as blueberries, raspberries, and blackberries

**1.** Preheat oven to 350°F. Line a standard 12-cup muffin tin with paper liners. In a medium bowl, whisk together cookie crumbs, flour, baking powder, and salt.

**2.** With an electric mixer on medium speed, beat butter with granulated sugar until pale and fluffy, about 1 minute. Beat in eggs, one at a time. Reduce speed to low and add flour mixture in three batches, alternating with milk, beginning and ending with flour mixture, and beating until just combined. Fold in coconut.

**3.** Divide batter evenly among prepared cups. Bake, rotating tin halfway through, until cupcakes are golden brown and centers bounce back when gently pressed, 22 to 24 minutes. Transfer pan to a wire rack to cool completely.

**4.** Add 2 tablespoons water to a small saucepan. Sprinkle with gelatin and let stand until thick, about 5 minutes. Gently heat over medium, stirring, until gelatin is dissolved. Remove from heat; let cool 5 minutes (but don't let it set).

**5.** With an electric mixer on medium speed, beat together cream, confectioners' sugar, and vanilla until very soft peaks form, about 2 minutes. Add gelatin mixture; beat on medium until stiff peaks form, about 1 minute more.

**6.** Turn out cupcakes from tin and arrange on a platter in a 3-by-4 rectangle. Spoon frosting over each row of cupcakes; using an offset spatula, smooth to cover tops, forming a rectangular shape. Refrigerate at least 1 hour and up to 3 hours. Sprinkle with berries before serving. (Cupcakes can be refrigerated, in an airtight container, up to 3 days.)

# Mini Spiced Cupcakes

## MAKES 4 DOZEN MINI CUPCAKES

*These little bites of sweet-spicy cake are all the more enticing when glazed in a rainbow of cheerful colors, as we've done here. Simply divide the glaze into small bowls and stir one or two drops of food coloring into each.*
*Depending on the occasion, you can go for bright hues or a softer pastel palette.*

### FOR THE CUPCAKES

2 sticks (1 cup) unsalted butter, room temperature, plus more for pans

1½ cups unbleached all-purpose flour

1½ teaspoons kosher salt

½ teaspoon ground cinnamon

½ teaspoon ground nutmeg

¼ teaspoon ground cardamom

1 cup packed light-brown sugar

2 large eggs, room temperature

½ cup whole milk

### FOR THE GLAZE

4 tablespoons fresh orange juice

1¾ cups confectioners' sugar, sifted

Gel-paste food coloring in various colors

**1. Make the cupcakes:** Preheat oven to 350°F with racks in upper and lower thirds. Lightly butter 48 mini-muffin cups. In a medium bowl, whisk together flour, salt, cinnamon, nutmeg, and cardamom.

**2.** With an electric mixer on medium-high speed, beat butter and brown sugar until light and fluffy, about 3 minutes. Add eggs, one at a time, beating well after each addition and scraping down sides of bowl as needed. Reduce speed to low. Add flour mixture in three batches, alternating with two additions of milk, beginning and ending with flour, and beating well after each addition.

**3.** Divide batter evenly among prepared cups. Bake, rotating tins halfway through, until golden brown at edges and a cake tester comes out clean, about 15 minutes. Transfer tins to wire racks to cool 10 minutes. Turn out cupcakes onto rack to cool completely. (Store unglazed cakes, tightly covered, at room temperature for up to 5 days; glaze before serving.)

**4. Make the glaze:** In a bowl, whisk together juice and confectioners' sugar until smooth; divide glaze into multiple bowls, adding 1 or 2 drops of gel as desired. Spoon over cooled cakes. (Cupcakes can be refrigerated, in an airtight container, up to 3 days.)

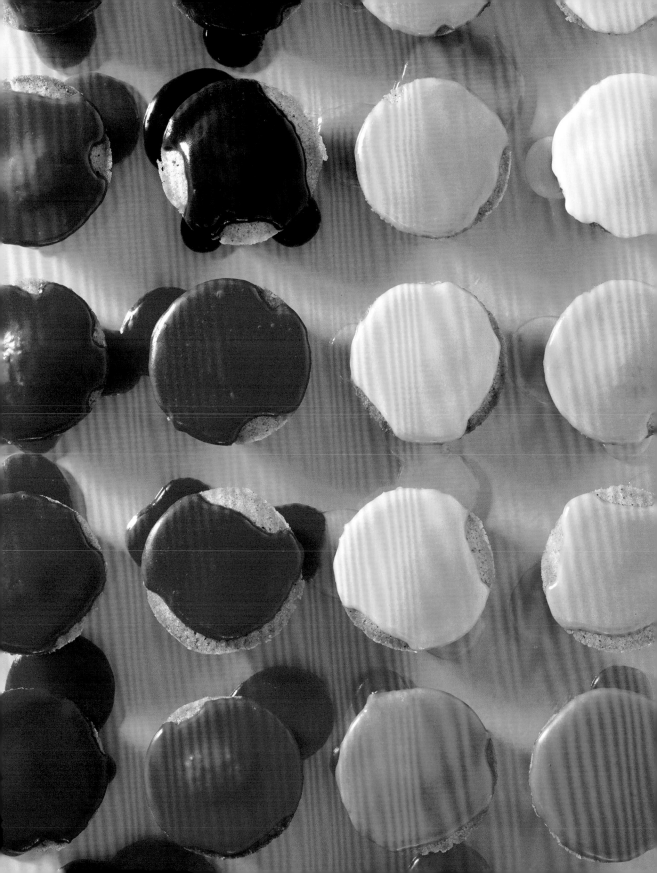

# Chocolate Stout Cupcakes

**MAKES 2 DOZEN**

*Everybody's favorite pub snack just got a sweet makeover: beer—
in this case, a nice dark stout like Guinness—and pretzels, in cupcake form.
The cakes are baked in a popover pan for extra height, and
cream cheese frosting provides the essential foamy head. Cheers!*

## FOR THE CUPCAKES

2 cups safflower oil, plus more

1¾ cups unsweetened
Dutch-process cocoa powder,
sifted, plus more for pan

4 cups unbleached
all-purpose flour

1 tablespoon baking soda

2 teaspoons kosher salt

2 bottles (11.2 ounces each)
dark stout, such as Guinness

¾ cup unsulfured molasses

4 large eggs, room temperature

2 cups granulated sugar

1 cup packed dark-brown sugar

1 tablespoon vanilla extract

1½ cups sour cream

Pretzels, crushed, for garnish

## FOR THE FROSTING

2 packages (8 ounces
each) cream cheese,
room temperature

2 sticks (1 cup) unsalted
butter, cut into pieces,
room temperature

2 tablespoons sour cream

2 cups confectioners'
sugar, sifted

½ teaspoon unsweetened
Dutch-process cocoa powder

2 teaspoons vanilla extract

**1. Make the cupcakes:** Preheat oven to 350°F. Grease 24 standard popover cups and dust with cocoa, tapping out any excess. In a large bowl, whisk together flour, baking soda, and salt. In another large bowl, whisk stout, molasses, and cocoa until smooth.

**2.** With an electric mixer on medium-high speed, beat eggs and both sugars until combined, 2 to 3 minutes. Reduce speed to low, and gradually beat in stout mixture. Increase speed to medium, and beat until combined. Reduce speed to low again, and beat in oil and vanilla. Add flour mixture in three batches, alternating with sour cream, beginning and ending with flour, and beating until combined.

**3.** Divide batter evenly among prepared cups, filling each about three-quarters full. Gently tap on the counter (batter will still look bubbly). Bake, rotating cups halfway through, until a cake tester comes out clean, about 20 minutes. Transfer pan to a wire rack to cool completely. Turn cakes out from pan and, using a serrated knife, trim rounded tops to create a flat surface.

**4. Make the frosting:** In a medium bowl, beat cream cheese with an electric mixer on medium speed until softened, 2 to 3 minutes. Gradually beat in butter and sour cream until smooth and well blended. Add confectioners' sugar and cocoa, and continue beating until smooth. Add vanilla and mix to combine.

**5.** Spoon about 3 tablespoons frosting on each cupcake, smoothing top edges with an offset spatula. Garnish each with crumbled pretzels. (Cupcakes are best eaten the day they are baked.)

# Mini Mocha Cupcakes

MAKES ABOUT 90 MINI CUPCAKES

*Serve these bite-size treats at a party or large gathering: The coffee-infused chocolate cake, chocolate mousse, and creamy ganache glaze join forces to create the ultimate mocha moment. Make the mousse and glaze (we used bittersweet chocolate) just before assembling the cupcakes.*

## FOR THE CUPCAKES

2 sticks (1 cup) plus 2 tablespoons unsalted butter, room temperature, plus more

1 cup plus 2 tablespoons unsweetened Dutch-process cocoa powder, plus more

2½ cups plus 2 tablespoons unbleached all-purpose flour

2 teaspoons baking soda

⅛ teaspoon kosher salt

1 cup granulated sugar

1 cup packed dark-brown sugar

3 large eggs, room temperature

¾ cup sour cream

1½ cups buttermilk

## FOR THE COFFEE SYRUP

½ cup granulated sugar

¼ cup coffee extract, such as Trablit

## FOR THE CHOCOLATE MOUSSE

1½ cups cold heavy cream

8 ounces bittersweet chocolate (70% cacao), melted

Chocolate Ganache Glaze (see page 241)

Coffee beans, crushed, for garnish

**1. Make the cupcakes:** Preheat oven to 350°F. Butter mini tins and dust with cocoa, tapping out excess. In a medium bowl, whisk together cocoa, flour, baking soda, and salt.

**2.** With an electric mixer on medium-high speed, beat butter and both sugars until pale and fluffy. Add eggs, one at a time, beating well after each addition and scraping down sides of bowl as needed. Mix in sour cream. Reduce speed to low and add flour mixture in three batches, alternating with buttermilk and beginning and ending with flour, until just combined.

**3.** Divide batter evenly among prepared mini cups, filling each about three-quarters full. Bake, rotating tins halfway through, until firm to the touch and a cake tester comes out clean, 8 to 10 minutes. Transfer tins to wire racks to cool 5 minutes. Turn out cupcakes onto racks to cool completely.

**4. Make the coffee syrup:** In a small saucepan, cook ½ cup water and granulated sugar over medium heat until sugar is dissolved and liquid begins to simmer. Stir in extract. (Refrigerate until ready to use.)

**5. Make the chocolate mousse:** In a chilled medium bowl, whisk cream until soft peaks form. Pour in melted chocolate; fold to incorporate. Refrigerate until just cool, about 10 minutes (if you overchill, it will stiffen too much). Place in a pastry bag fitted with a large plain tip.

**6.** Halve cupcakes horizontally. Brush bottom (and top for stronger flavor) with coffee syrup. Pipe 2 teaspoons mousse onto each bottom. Dip tops in chocolate ganache glaze and set on top of mousse. Garnish with crushed coffee beans. (Cupcakes can be refrigerated, in an airtight container, up to 3 days.)

# Citrus Swirl Cupcakes

### MAKES 2 DOZEN

*Pretty pastels, soft-serve style—what could be sweeter? Tint the frosting*
*to match the citrus—yellow for lemon, green for lime, orange for orange. Choose one flavor*
*to keep it simple, or decorate with all three as we did here. To achieve*
*a lofty swirl, hold the piping bag vertically and pipe in one continual movement.*

---

**FOR THE CUPCAKES**

3 cups unbleached
all-purpose flour

1½ teaspoons baking powder

¾ teaspoon kosher salt

1½ sticks (¾ cup) unsalted
butter, room temperature

1½ cups sugar

2 tablespoons lemon,
lime, or orange zest

4 large eggs, room temperature

2 teaspoons vanilla extract

1 cup plus 2 tablespoons
whole milk

2 tablespoons freshly
squeezed lemon, lime, or
orange juice

**FOR THE BUTTERCREAM**

2½ cups sugar

10 large egg whites,
room temperature

8 sticks (4 cups) unsalted
butter, cut into pieces,
room temperature

2 teaspoons vanilla extract

Gel-paste food
coloring in yellow,
lime green, and orange

**1. Make the cupcakes:** Preheat oven to 350°F. Line two standard 12-cup muffin tins with paper liners. In a medium bowl, whisk together flour, baking powder, and salt. With an electric mixer on medium-high speed, beat butter, sugar, and citrus zest until light and fluffy. Reduce speed to medium. Add eggs, one at a time, beating well and scraping down sides of bowl as needed. Beat in vanilla. In a small bowl, whisk together milk and citrus juice. Reduce speed to low and add flour mixture in three batches, alternating with milk mixture.

**2.** Divide batter evenly among prepared cups, filling each about three-quarters full. Bake, rotating tins halfway through, until tops spring back when touched, about 20 minutes. Transfer tins to a wire rack to cool 5 minutes. Turn out cupcakes on rack to cool completely.

**3. Make the buttercream:** In a heatproof bowl set over (not in) a pan of gently simmering water, whisk sugar and egg whites until sugar dissolves and egg whites are hot to the touch, about 3 minutes. With an electric mixer, whisk on high speed until mixture cools completely and forms stiff, glossy peaks, about 10 minutes. Reduce speed to medium. Add butter, a few pieces at a time; beat until incorporated. Add vanilla and beat just until combined. Switch to paddle attachment and beat on lowest speed to eliminate any air pockets, about 5 minutes.

**4.** Divide buttercream into 6 small bowls. (If decorating in a single color, divide buttercream into 2 bowls.) Add gel, a drop at a time, to 3 bowls until desired shades of yellow, lime green, and orange are reached. Place each buttercream (including plain buttercream) into a pastry bag and snip end. For each color, place a tinted bag and a plain bag of buttercream side by side in a large pastry bag fitted with a large round tip (such as Ateco #808). Hold bag vertically and pipe in one continual swirling fashion. Release pressure as you quickly lift up tip. (Cupcakes can be refrigerated, in an airtight container, up to 3 days; bring to room temperature before serving.)

# Chocolate Pudding Cupcakes

**MAKES 18**

*These were inspired by those of our youth: a chocolate base filled with creamy chocolate pudding and topped with an easy chocolate ganache glaze. A chocolate curl on top completes the perfect bite.*

**FOR THE PUDDING**

¼ cup sugar

2 tablespoons plus 1 teaspoon cornstarch

1 tablespoon unsweetened Dutch-process cocoa powder

¼ teaspoon kosher salt

1¼ cups whole milk

1 large egg yolk

1 teaspoon vanilla extract

3 ounces milk chocolate, coarsely chopped (⅔ cup)

**FOR THE CUPCAKES**

2 cups unbleached all-purpose flour

2 teaspoons baking powder

1½ teaspoons kosher salt

1½ sticks (¾ cup) unsalted butter, room temperature

1⅓ cups sugar

3 large eggs, room temperature

1½ teaspoons vanilla extract

¾ cup whole milk

5 ounces bittersweet chocolate (61 to 70% cacao), melted and cooled

Chocolate Ganache Glaze (page 241)

½ block of good-quality chocolate

**1. Make the chocolate pudding:** In a medium saucepan, whisk together sugar, cornstarch, cocoa, and salt. Whisk in milk and egg yolk. Bring to a boil over medium-high, whisking constantly; cook until thickened, about 2 minutes. Remove from heat; whisk in vanilla and chopped chocolate until melted. Pour mixture into a bowl and cover with plastic wrap, pressing it directly onto surface. Refrigerate until cold, at least 30 minutes and up to overnight.

**2. Make the cupcakes:** Preheat oven to 350°F. Line two standard 12-cup muffin tins with 18 paper liners. Whisk together flour, baking powder, and salt in a large bowl.

**3.** In a separate large bowl, beat butter and sugar with an electric mixer on medium speed until light and fluffy. Add eggs, one at a time, beating well after each addition. Beat in vanilla. Reduce speed to low and add flour mixture in two batches, alternating with milk and beginning and ending with flour. Beat in melted chocolate.

**4.** Divide batter evenly among prepared cups, filling each about two-thirds full. Bake until a cake tester comes out clean, 18 to 20 minutes. Transfer pan to a wire rack to cool 5 minutes. Turn out cupcakes onto rack to cool completely. (Cupcakes can be made ahead up to this point and stored in an airtight container at room temperature up to 2 days.)

**5.** Transfer pudding to a pastry bag fitted with a ¼-inch plain round tip. Insert tip in top of a cupcake and squeeze until cupcake begins to mound. Repeat with remaining cupcakes. Refrigerate until cold, at least 30 minutes and up to 1 day.

**6.** Spoon about 2 teaspoons ganache over each cupcake. Using a vegetable peeler, slice strips of chocolate onto each cupcake. Refrigerate at least 15 minutes before serving.

**DECORATING TIP**
Gel-paste food colorings develop and darken over time, so start with lighter colors when tinting frosting.

# Succulent Matcha Cupcakes

**MAKES 1 DOZEN**

*With a steady hand and some basic piping techniques, you can produce a veritable garden of edible succulents atop these green-tea-flavored cakes. Follow the decorating tips on page 192, practice on parchment before you get started, and use a flower nail (available at baking-supply stores) for best results.*

1 cup cake flour
(not self-rising)

4 teaspoons matcha powder

½ teaspoon baking powder

¼ teaspoon baking soda

¼ teaspoon kosher salt

4 tablespoons unsalted
butter, room temperature

¾ cup sugar

1 large egg,
room temperature

½ cup whole milk

Swiss Meringue
Buttercream (page 237)

Gel-paste food coloring
in mint green, leaf green,
forest green, dark purple,
light brown, and peach

**1.** Preheat oven to 350°F. Line a standard 12-cup muffin tin with paper liners. In a medium bowl, whisk together flour, matcha, baking powder, baking soda, and salt.

**2.** With an electric mixer on high speed, beat butter and sugar until light and fluffy, about 3 minutes, scraping down sides of bowl as needed. Reduce speed to medium. Add egg and mix until just combined. Reduce speed to low and add flour mixture in batches, alternating with milk, until combined.

**3.** Divide batter evenly among prepared cups, filling each about halfway. Bake, rotating tin halfway through, until cupcakes spring back to the touch and a cake tester comes out clean, about 16 minutes. Transfer tin to a wire rack to cool 5 minutes. Turn out cupcakes onto rack and let cool completely.

**4.** Divide buttercream into 5 bowls, reserving a few tablespoons of plain. Add gel-paste food coloring to bowls, a drop at a time, to achieve desired shades of mint green, leaf green, forest green, dark purple, and light brown. (Make more of the shade you'll want to spread on the base of your cupcakes.)

**5.** Using a star tip, pipe vertical mounds of varying thickness to create cactus shapes. Use a very small round tip to pipe white dots along the sides or use a very small star tip to pipe a flower on top. To make the small individual succulents, pipe onto a flower nail and then transfer to the cupcake. See page 192 for decorating details. (Cupcakes are best eaten the day they are baked.)

*(continued on page 192)*

*To create the succulents shown opposite, follow the steps below. Use a flower nail (we used a #7), available at baking-supply stores. Adhere a small square of parchment to the surface of the flower nail with a dab of frosting. Pipe the design, then gently slide the parchment off the nail onto a baking sheet and refrigerate about 20 minutes. Use a small offset spatula to transfer the designs to the cupcakes. To make them two-toned in color, paint stripes of one color of buttercream along the inside of the piping bag, then fill the bag with a second color buttercream.*

## 1.

Using a small petal tip (such as #104), squeeze the bag gently and pull up slowly to make an acorn shape on top of the parchment. Holding the tip against the point of the acorn, wide end down and the narrow end angled in toward the acorn's center, pipe a wide strip as you turn the nail, enrobing the top completely. Continue turning the nail, making longer petals that overlap.

## 2.

Using a medium petal tip (such as #125), pipe a basic petal: Hold the bag at a 45-degree angle to the surface, with the tip's wide end down and the narrow end pointed away slightly to the left. Move the tip forward and back again while you pivot the narrow end to the right, creating a long fan-shaped petal.

Pipe additional petals, overlapping each one slightly. Using the same petal technique, pipe smaller petals.

## 3.

Using a U-shaped petal tip (such as #80 or #81), pipe a dot about ½ inch in diameter to form the base. Hold the bag at a 45-degree angle against the edge of the dot, with the tip's U shape facing up. Apply pressure, squeezing the bag, while pulling out in a quick stroke. Repeat all around the dot; form three or more petal layers over the first, making petals shorter with each layer.

## 4.

Using a fine leaf tip (such as #352), pipe a small mound in the center of a flower nail to form the base. Holding the tip vertically against the surface, with the pointed end of the leaf tip almost touching the mound, apply gentle steady pressure as you pipe a leaf-shaped petal. Then decrease pressure as you pull away. Repeat with more leaf-shaped petals around the base of the center mound. Add more layers of petals until the entire mound is covered, making the petals shorter as you reach the top.

## 5.

Using a small open star tip (such as #199) and holding the bag at a 90-degree angle to the surface, squeeze the bag with steady pressure. Then stop pressure and pull away when you have reached the desired height of barrel cacti. To create needles, use white frosting and a fine tip (such as #1 or #2) and pipe small dots along the spines. Use peach frosting to pipe blossoms on the top of the cacti.

# 6

# Celebration
# Cakes

*Whether you're basking in the yuletide glow, baking
up some Valentine love, or breaking out the sprinkles for
a birthday bash, we have a dessert to honor the
occasion. Each one is infused with seasonal flavors
and will help get the celebration started.*

———————

# Spring Nest Cake

### MAKES ONE 9-INCH LAYER CAKE

*Welcome spring or Easter with this pastel-frosted cake—topped with a treat-filled chocolate nest. To make the nest, we relied on a chocolatiers' technique: Freeze vodka in a baking pan, then pipe melted chocolate into the liquid in the shape of a circle. Voilà! Your nest is built. If only momma birds had it that easy.*

---

## FOR THE BUTTERCREAM

3 sticks (1½ cups) unsalted butter, room temperature

1 pound confectioners' sugar, sifted (about 4 cups)

½ teaspoon vanilla extract

Gel-paste food coloring in lavender

Two 9-inch layer cakes (see Mix-and-Match Cakes, page 226)

## FOR THE NEST

3 cups vodka

8 ounces bittersweet chocolate (70% cacao), chopped (1½ cups)

Candies, for filling nest

**1. Make the buttercream:** In a large bowl, beat butter with an electric mixer on medium-high speed until pale and creamy, about 2 minutes. Reduce speed to medium and add confectioners' sugar, ½ cup at a time, beating well after each addition. (After every two additions, increase speed to high and beat 10 seconds, then reduce speed to medium again.) Add vanilla and beat until buttercream is smooth. Add gel, a drop at a time, until desired shade is reached. (Use immediately, or cover and refrigerate up to 3 days. Bring to room temperature, and beat on low speed until smooth before using.)

**2.** With a serrated knife, trim tops of cake layers to level. Transfer a cake layer, bottom-side down, to a cake stand lined with parchment strips. Spread 1 cup frosting evenly over cake layer. Place second layer, bottom-side up, on top. Spread a thin layer of frosting over cake to form a crumb coat; refrigerate until firm, about 30 minutes. Spread 2 cups frosting evenly over top and sides. Using a large offset spatula or a bench scraper, set an edge against the side of the cake and, spinning cake stand evenly, smooth frosting.

**3. Make the nest:** Pour vodka into an 8-inch cake pan. Freeze until very cold, at least 30 minutes. Meanwhile, in a heatproof bowl set over (not in) a pot of boiling water, melt chocolate, stirring until smooth. Let cool slightly, then transfer to a pastry bag; snip off a very small piece of end. Drizzle chocolate into cold vodka in a circular motion, stopping after a few rings form. Using two forks, transfer chocolate rings to a paper towel–lined plate. Repeat with remaining chocolate, layering rings to build a nest shape. Refrigerate until nest is firm enough to lift and condensation evaporates, about 30 minutes. Carefully place nest atop cake and nestle candies inside.

**DECORATING TIP**

For straighter lines in
your nest, pipe in smooth,
consistent circles;
go slower for more
organic, wiggly lines.

**BAKING TIP**

We chose matzo cake meal for this chiffon, as it is more finely ground than matzo meal, with a texture that works better for a finer crumb.

# Coconut Chiffon Cake

MAKES ONE 10-INCH CAKE

*Celebrate Passover with this airy chiffon cake, which is leavened only by whipped egg whites and enriched with coconut oil rather than butter. The frosting should be pourable; if it gets too thick, microwave it for ten seconds at a time to thin it before pouring it over the cake and topping with toasted coconut.*

---

⅔ cup matzo cake meal

⅔ cup potato starch

½ teaspoon kosher salt

8 large eggs, separated, room temperature

1½ cups superfine sugar

1 vanilla bean, split and seeds scraped

6 tablespoons unrefined virgin coconut oil (3 ounces), melted

½ cup full-fat coconut milk

4 ounces bittersweet chocolate (70% cacao), chopped (¾ cup)

¾ cup unsweetened coconut flakes, toasted

**1.** Preheat oven to 350°F. In a small bowl, whisk together matzo cake meal, potato starch, and salt. In a large bowl, beat egg whites with an electric mixer on medium-high speed to soft peaks. Gradually add ¾ cup sugar and beat until stiff, glossy peaks form.

**2.** In another large bowl, beat egg yolks with an electric mixer on medium-high speed with remaining ¾ cup sugar and the vanilla seeds until pale and doubled in volume, about 5 minutes. Gradually beat in 3 tablespoons oil, then coconut milk, just until combined. Add matzo mixture and beat just until combined. Stir in one-third of egg whites, then gently fold in remaining whites in two additions, just until combined and no streaks remain (do not overmix). Transfer batter to an ungreased 10-inch tube pan (preferably footed) with a removable bottom, smoothing top with an offset spatula.

**3.** Bake cake until golden on top and a cake tester comes out clean, 40 to 45 minutes. Invert pan and let cool completely; if pan is not footed, invert center of tube onto the neck of a bottle to allow air circulation.

**4.** Turn cake right-side up. Run a thin, sharp knife around sides of pan and center tube. Lift cake by center tube; remove ring. Run knife around bottom of pan to loosen; invert cake to remove. Place on a plate or stand.

**5.** Prepare an ice-water bath. Combine remaining 3 tablespoons oil and the chocolate in a bowl set over (not in) a pot of simmering water; stir until melted. Remove from heat and set in ice-water bath, stirring constantly, until thickened slightly but still pourable, 1 to 2 minutes. Pour frosting evenly over top and sprinkle with coconut. Cut into wedges and serve.

# Banana Heart Cake

### SERVES 12

*We looked to one of Martha's Good Things ideas for a distinctive heart shape: Instead of buying a specialty mold, bake the banana cake in an everyday 8-inch round and 8-inch square. Slice the round in half, placing the halves on two adjacent sides of the square to form a heart. A coconut topping in three shades of pink takes this to a swoon-worthy level.*

---

1 stick (½ cup) plus
2 tablespoons unsalted
butter, room temperature,
plus more for pan

2 cups unbleached all-purpose
flour, plus more for pan

1¼ teaspoons baking powder

¾ teaspoon baking soda

½ teaspoon kosher salt

2¼ very ripe medium
bananas, mashed

3 tablespoons sour cream

¾ teaspoon vanilla extract

1¼ cups plus
2 tablespoons sugar

3 large eggs,
room temperature

4 cups unsweetened
coconut flakes

Powdered food coloring or
luster dust in 3 shades of pink

Cream Cheese
Frosting (page 240)

**1.** Preheat oven to 350°F. Butter one 8-inch round cake pan and one 8-inch square cake pan. Line with parchment paper; butter parchment. Dust with flour, tapping out any excess. In a medium bowl, whisk together flour, baking powder, baking soda, and salt. In a small bowl, stir together mashed banana, sour cream, and vanilla; set aside.

**2.** In a medium bowl, with an electric mixer on medium speed, beat together butter and sugar until light and fluffy, 3 to 4 minutes, scraping down the sides of the bowl as needed. Add eggs, one at a time, beating well after each addition. Reduce speed to low and add reserved banana mixture, beating until combined. Add flour mixture in two batches, beating until just combined after each addition, 2 to 3 minutes.

**3.** Divide batter evenly between prepared pans, smoothing tops with an offset spatula. Bake, rotating pans halfway through, until cakes are golden brown and a cake tester comes out clean, 30 to 35 minutes. Transfer pans to a wire rack to cool 20 minutes. Turn out cakes onto rack to cool completely.

**4.** Divide coconut flakes evenly among three resealable plastic bags. Add about ¼ teaspoon powdered food coloring to each bag; seal and shake to coat coconut. (For a more saturated color, add up to an additional ¼ teaspoon powdered food coloring.)

**5.** With a serrated knife, split round cake layer in half vertically to form 2 semicircles. Place square cake layer on a large cake board, serving platter, or cutting board so that one corner is oriented toward you, making a diamond shape. Spread about ¼ cup frosting along the top two edges of diamond, then position each semicircle against a frosted edge of diamond, making a heart-shaped cake. Spread remaining frosting generously over entire cake. Sprinkle top and sides with tinted coconut flakes, covering completely.

**STORING TIP**

You can store this
cake, wrapped tightly
in plastic, in
the refrigerator
up to 3 days.

# Chocolate-Raspberry Cake

### MAKES ONE 8-INCH LAYER CAKE

*Some flavor pairings are meant to be. So for Valentine's Day, we decided to honor one of our favorite love matches—chocolate and raspberry. A heady touch of raspberry liqueur goes into the batter, then, while the layers bake, whip up a luscious berry-rich filling. The result? Romance on a plate.*

**FOR THE CAKE**

Vegetable-oil cooking spray

1½ cups unbleached all-purpose flour

¼ cup unsweetened Dutch-process cocoa powder

¾ teaspoon baking soda

1 teaspoon kosher salt

1½ sticks (¾ cup) unsalted butter, room temperature

1¼ cups sugar

3 large eggs, room temperature

1 tablespoon raspberry liqueur, such as Chambord or framboise

1 cup buttermilk, room temperature

4 ounces bittersweet chocolate (61 to 70% cacao) melted and cooled

**FOR THE FILLING**

4 packages (6 ounces each) fresh raspberries (a scant 6 cups)

¾ cup plus 2 tablespoons sugar

Pinch of kosher salt

2 teaspoons fresh lemon juice

Chocolate Frosting (page 240)

**1. Make the cake:** Preheat oven to 350°F. Lightly coat three 8-by-2-inch round cake pans with cooking spray; line with parchment. In a large bowl, whisk together flour, cocoa, baking soda, and salt. In another large bowl, beat butter and sugar with an electric mixer on high speed until light and fluffy, about 3 minutes. Add eggs, one at a time, beating well after each addition. Beat in liqueur, if desired. Reduce speed to low and add flour mixture in three batches, alternating with buttermilk and beginning and ending with flour. Beat to combine, scraping down sides of bowl as needed. Beat in melted chocolate.

**2.** Divide batter evenly among prepared pans, smoothing tops with an offset spatula. Bake, rotating pans halfway through, until a cake tester comes out clean, about 25 minutes. Transfer pans to a wire rack to cool 10 minutes. Run a small sharp knife around edges, then turn out cakes onto rack to cool completely.

**3. Make the filling:** In a medium saucepan, stir together 3 cups raspberries, the sugar, salt, and lemon juice. Cook over high heat, stirring frequently and mashing with the back of a spoon, until mixture comes to a boil, about 2 minutes. Continue to cook, stirring, until mixture thickens and clings to spoon, 7 to 8 minutes more. (You should have about 1⅓ cups.) Let cool about 30 minutes. Stir in 2 cups raspberries, reserving remainder.

**4.** With a serrated knife, trim tops of cake layers to level. Transfer one layer, trimmed-side up, to a cake plate or stand lined with parchment. Spread half the filling over cake layer. Top with second layer; spread remaining filling over top. Top with final layer, trimmed-side down. Spread a thin layer of frosting over top and sides to create a crumb coat. Refrigerate, covered, at least 1 hour and up to overnight. Spread frosting over top and sides of cake. Garnish with remaining raspberries.

# Chocolate Heart Cupcakes

**MAKES 1 DOZEN**

*Bake your Valentine a message of love with these heart-cutout cupcakes. The decorating step couldn't be more charming: Carve out a space with a heart-shaped cutter to pipe the vanilla milk frosting in half the cakes, then frost the other half and use the cutouts as toppers. Cherry juice helps keep the cakes tender and deepens the chocolate flavor.*

---

1¼ cups unbleached all-purpose flour

¾ teaspoon baking powder

½ teaspoon kosher salt

¼ teaspoon baking soda

⅔ cup sugar

⅓ cup unsweetened Dutch-process cocoa powder

2 ounces semisweet chocolate, finely chopped (½ cup)

½ cup unsweetened pure cherry or pomegranate juice

1 stick (½ cup) plus 2 tablespoons unsalted butter

2 large eggs, room temperature

Vanilla-Bean Milk Frosting (page 242)

**1.** Preheat oven to 325°F. Line a 12-cup standard muffin tin with paper liners. In a medium bowl, whisk together flour, baking powder, salt, and baking soda. In a large heatproof bowl, whisk together sugar, cocoa, and chocolate. Whisk in cherry juice.

**2.** In a small saucepan over medium heat, melt butter, then continue to simmer until bubbles recede and solids on bottom of pan begin to turn golden brown, about 6 minutes. Pour into sugar mixture; whisk until well combined and chocolate melts. Whisk in eggs. Add flour mixture and fold to combine.

**3.** Divide batter evenly among prepared cups. Bake until tops spring back when lightly touched, 22 to 24 minutes. Transfer tin to a wire rack to cool 5 minutes. Turn out cupcakes on rack to cool completely. Refrigerate at least 2 hours and up to 12 (this will help create clean cuts).

**4.** Use a 1½-inch heart-shaped cutter to remove a ¾-inch-deep heart from each of 6 cupcakes (remove a bit of additional cake, if desired, to create more room for frosting); set aside. Fill a pastry bag fitted with a large, plain round tip (such as Ateco #806) with frosting. Pipe frosting to fill heart cutouts. Pipe ¼ cup frosting evenly on remaining cupcakes, and top with reserved heart cutouts. (Cupcakes can be stored in an airtight container at room temperature up to 2 days.)

# Citrus-and-Spice Cheesecake

## SERVES 10

*Ring in the New Year with a dazzling cake that's all gemstone colors and sophisticated shine. The shingled fruit—a mix of grapefruit and Cara Cara, navel, and blood oranges—creates a rainbow effect: Just section the fruit (suprêming each piece—removing its membrane—for the cleanest look), then layer by color.*

---

1 stick (½ cup) unsalted butter, melted, plus more for pan

12 graham cracker sheets, ground into fine crumbs (1½ cups)

1 cup plus 3 tablespoons sugar

2 packages (8 ounces each) cream cheese, room temperature

½ cup sour cream, room temperature

1 teaspoon ground ginger

⅛ teaspoon ground allspice

Pinch of kosher salt

2 large eggs, lightly beaten, room temperature

Mixed citrus–fruit, such as grapefruit, Cara Cara oranges, navel oranges, and/or blood oranges

1¼ teaspoons unflavored powdered gelatin (from 1 envelope)

¼ cup fresh lemon juice (from 2 lemons)

**1.** Preheat oven to 350°F. Butter a 10-inch springform pan. In a bowl, combine graham cracker crumbs, 2 tablespoons sugar, and the melted butter; press into bottom of pan. Bake until firm, about 10 minutes. Transfer pan to a wire rack to cool completely. Reduce oven to 325°F.

**2.** Bring a kettle of water to a boil. With an electric mixer on medium speed, beat cream cheese and sour cream until smooth. Beat in ¾ cup sugar, the ginger, allspice, and salt. Add eggs and beat until smooth.

**3.** Wrap bottom half of springform pan in foil. Place pan in a roasting pan and pour filling over crust. Transfer to oven and pour in boiling water until it's halfway up sides of pan. Bake until cake is just set in center, 35 to 40 minutes. Transfer pan to a wire rack to cool completely. Refrigerate until firm, at least 1 hour and up to 1 day.

**4. Suprême citrus:** Using a sharp knife and a cutting board, trim both ends of fruit. Set fruit on a trimmed end. Beginning at top and following curves of fruit, remove peel and pith. Working over a medium bowl to catch juice, carefully cut between membranes to release segments. Squeeze remaining membrane to extract juice, reserving for another use; discard membrane.

**5.** In a small bowl, sprinkle gelatin over ¼ cup cold water; let soften 1 minute. In a small saucepan over medium heat, combine remaining ⅓ cup sugar, the lemon juice, and 1 cup water; cook, stirring, until sugar is dissolved. Remove from heat and stir in gelatin until dissolved.

**6.** Arrange citrus segments over cake. Gently pour gelatin mixture on top. Refrigerate overnight.

**7.** To serve, unmold cheesecake onto a platter. Cut into slices with a serrated knife, using a sawing motion to cut citrus segments and wiping knife between cuts.

# Coffee-Caramel Swiss Roll

### SERVES 8 TO 10

*Like most Swiss rolls, this bûche de Noël starts with sponge cake.
Ours is brushed with espresso syrup to flavor the cake and help it roll easily
around the lush caramel filling. After enrobing the roll in long
swoops of seven-minute frosting, use a kitchen torch for a faux bois finish.*

---

## FOR THE CAKE

¼ cup safflower oil,
plus more for pan

1¼ cups cake flour
(not self–rising)

½ teaspoon kosher salt

1¼ teaspoons baking powder

⅓ cup hot water

¾ cup granulated sugar

5 large eggs, separated,
room temperature

1 teaspoon vanilla extract

Pinch of cream of tartar

Confectioners' sugar,
sifted, for dusting

## FOR THE SYRUP

¼ cup granulated sugar

1 tablespoon instant
espresso powder

## FOR THE FILLING

6 tablespoons
granulated sugar

¼ teaspoon kosher salt

1½ cups heavy cream

Seven-Minute
Frosting (page 238)

**1. Make the cake:** Preheat oven to 350°F. Brush a 12½-by-17½-inch rimmed baking sheet with oil. Line bottom with parchment; oil parchment.

**2.** In a medium bowl, whisk together flour, salt, and baking powder. In a large heatproof bowl, whisk hot water with ½ cup granulated sugar until dissolved. Whisk in oil, then egg yolks and vanilla until smooth. Whisk flour mixture into sugar mixture just until combined. In a large bowl, beat egg whites with an electric mixer on medium-low speed until frothy. Add cream of tartar, increase speed to medium-high, and continue beating until soft peaks form. Gradually add remaining ¼ cup granulated sugar, and continue beating until stiff, glossy peaks form. Stir one-third of egg whites into batter. Gently fold in remaining egg whites just until no white streaks remain. Transfer batter to prepared sheet; spread evenly to edges with an offset spatula.

**3.** Bake until pale golden, pulling away from edges, and top springs back when lightly touched, 17 to 19 minutes. Transfer sheet to a wire rack to cool 5 minutes. Meanwhile, generously dust a clean kitchen towel with confectioners' sugar. Flip cake out onto towel, remove parchment, and generously dust top with more confectioners' sugar. Starting at one short end, roll up cake in towel. Let cool completely, about 1 hour.

*(continued on page 210)*

**4. Make the syrup:** In a small saucepan, bring granulated sugar and 3 tablespoons water to a boil, stirring until dissolved. Remove from heat; whisk in espresso powder until dissolved (mixture will foam). Transfer to a heatproof bowl and refrigerate until cold, about 30 minutes.

**5. Make the filling:** Prepare an ice-water bath. In a medium saucepan, combine granulated sugar, 1 tablespoon water, and the salt. Cover; cook over medium heat, swirling a few times, until mixture boils and sugar dissolves, about 5 minutes. Uncover and continue boiling, undisturbed, until mixture turns golden amber, 3 to 5 minutes more. Remove from heat. Carefully add cream in a slow, steady stream (it will splatter). Return to medium heat and cook, stirring, until smooth. Transfer to a bowl set in an ice-water bath; let stand, stirring a few times, until cold, about 30 minutes. Remove from bath and whisk to stiff peaks.

**6.** Unroll cake. Brush any residual sugar from top, then brush evenly with espresso syrup. Dollop with filling, spreading it evenly with an offset spatula and leaving a ½-inch border. Starting at one short end, roll up cake (without towel). Wrap cake roll in towel and transfer to a baking sheet, seam-side down, to maintain cylindrical shape. Refrigerate until filling sets, at least 8 hours and up to 1 day.

**7.** Remove cake roll from towel; transfer to a serving platter. Spread frosting evenly over top and sides. (Frosted cake can be refrigerated, uncovered, up to 3 hours before slicing and serving.) Using a kitchen torch, move flame back and forth along meringue until golden brown. Slice cake into rounds and serve.

**BAKING TIP**

To prevent cracks in the cake, roll it while it is still warm and malleable, in a tea towel dusted with confectioners' sugar (use cocoa powder if the Swiss roll is chocolate).

# Disco Angel Cake

MAKES ONE 10-INCH CAKE

*When is angel food cake not so angelic? When it features two kinds of chocolate and gets dolled up with pink and gold. This decadent-but-still-light cake calls for cocoa powder in its egg-white-leavened batter, plus bittersweet chocolate in the frosting. Finish it with a smattering of nonpareils, sugar pearls, stars, and sprinkles.*

---

¼ cup unsweetened Dutch–process cocoa powder

1½ teaspoons instant espresso powder

¼ cup boiling water

1 tablespoon vanilla extract

1¾ cups sugar

1 cup cake flour (not self–rising)

½ teaspoon kosher salt

16 large egg whites, room temperature

1½ teaspoons cream of tartar

Double Chocolate Frosting (page 241)

Assorted edible nonpareils, dragées, sprinkles, and gold dust, for decorating

**1.** Preheat oven to 350°F. In a small bowl, whisk together cocoa, espresso, and boiling water until smooth. Whisk in vanilla. In a medium bowl, whisk together ¾ cup sugar, the cake flour, and salt.

**2.** In a large bowl, beat egg whites with an electric mixer on medium-low speed until frothy, about 2 minutes. Add cream of tartar, increase speed to medium, and continue beating until soft peaks form, 2 to 3 minutes. Increase speed to high and gradually add remaining 1 cup sugar, beating until stiff, glossy peaks form, about 5 minutes. Remove a heaping cup of meringue and whisk into cocoa mixture; set aside.

**3.** Gently transfer meringue to a large bowl. Sift flour mixture over meringue, ¼ cup at a time, gently folding in with a small rubber spatula until just combined. Fold cocoa-meringue mixture in until uniform and there are no streaks. Pour batter into an ungreased 10-inch tube pan. Run a small offset spatula through batter to dislodge any air pockets; smooth top. Bake until cake springs back when lightly pressed and a cake tester comes out clean, about 40 minutes. Invert pan; let cake cool completely in pan. Run a thin knife around inner and outer perimeter of tube pan to loosen cake; use knife to release cake.

**4.** Using a serrated knife, split cake in half horizontally. Transfer bottom layer to a cake stand. Spread ¾ cup frosting evenly over layer with an offset spatula. Top with second layer. Cover top and sides of cake with remaining frosting, using offset spatula to create either a smooth finish or swirls. Decorate with assorted edible nonpareils, dragées, sprinkles, and gold dust. Serve immediately.

# Sprinkle Cake

### MAKES ONE 8-INCH CAKE

*A three-layer cake, complete with homemade "confetti" sprinkles
inside and out, is what birthday dreams are made of. Take this opportunity
to make the sprinkles from scratch, so you can customize the
colors and keep the taste (essentially sugar and vanilla) simple and sublime.*

---

## FOR THE CAKE

1½ sticks (¾ cup)
unsalted butter,
room temperature,
plus more for pans

3 cups unbleached
all-purpose flour

1½ tablespoons
baking powder

¾ teaspoon kosher salt

2¼ cups granulated sugar

4 large eggs, room temperature

1½ teaspoons vanilla extract

1½ cups whole milk

¾ cup Homemade
Sprinkles (page 244), plus
more for decorating

## FOR THE FROSTING

2 sticks (1 cup) unsalted
butter, room temperature

Zest of 1 orange

6 to 8 cups confectioners'
sugar, sifted

½ cup whole milk

1 tablespoon vanilla extract

**1. Make the cake:** Preheat oven to 350°F. Butter three 8-inch cake pans. Line with parchment; butter parchment. Dust with flour, tapping out any excess. In a large bowl, whisk together flour, baking powder, and salt.

**2.** In a medium bowl, beat butter and sugar with an electric mixer on medium-high speed until light and fluffy, 3 to 5 minutes. Add eggs, one at a time, beating well after each addition and scraping down sides of bowl as needed. Beat in vanilla. Reduce speed to low and gradually add flour mixture in two batches, alternating with milk; mix until just combined. Fold sprinkles into batter using a rubber spatula.

**3.** Divide batter evenly among prepared pans, smoothing tops with an offset spatula. Bake until lightly golden and a cake tester comes out clean, 33 to 35 minutes. Transfer pans to wire racks to cool 15 minutes. Turn out cakes onto rack to cool completely.

**4. Make the frosting:** In a medium bowl, beat butter and orange zest with an electric mixer on medium-high speed until smooth, about 3 minutes. Reduce speed to low and gradually add 6 cups confectioners' sugar, along with the milk and vanilla; mix until smooth. Increase speed to medium-high and beat until light and fluffy, 3 to 5 minutes more. Gradually add more confectioners' sugar (up to 2 more cups), as needed, until a stiff but fluffy consistency is reached.

**5.** Use a dab of buttercream to anchor a cake layer to a cake board or stand. Spread a generous 1 cup frosting evenly over cake with an offset spatula. Sprinkle with 2 tablespoons sprinkles. Repeat process, ending with third cake layer, bottom-side up. Spread a thin layer of frosting over top and sides to create a crumb coat. Refrigerate about 15 minutes. Frost top and sides of cake with remaining buttercream. Transfer cake to refrigerator to chill, 15 to 30 minutes. To finish, lightly press remaining sprinkles by the handful onto the sides of the cake. (Leftover cake can be refrigerated up to 3 days; bring to room temperature before serving.)

**DECORATING TIP**

Coordinate the colors
of the homemade
sprinkles with your
party palette.

# Cranberry-Swirl Cheesecake

## SERVES 10

*Come Thanksgiving time, add some in-season elegance to a classic cheesecake—
with swirls of cranberry sauce you have waiting for the table
(either homemade or store-bought). Mark this on your prep list to make
the day before so the dessert has plenty of time to chill and set.*

---

8 graham crackers sheets, broken into pieces

2 tablespoons unsalted butter, melted

1¼ cups plus 2 tablespoons sugar

4 packages (8 ounces each) cream cheese, room temperature

¼ teaspoon kosher salt

1 teaspoon vanilla extract

4 large eggs, room temperature

1 cup whole-cranberry sauce

**1.** Preheat oven to 350°F. Wrap exterior of a 9-inch springform pan (including bottom) in a double layer of foil.

**2.** Pulse graham crackers in a food processor until finely ground. Add butter and 2 tablespoons sugar; pulse until mixture has the texture of wet sand. Press firmly into bottom of prepared pan. Bake until set and slightly darkened, 10 to 12 minutes. Transfer pan to a wire rack to cool completely.

**3.** Reduce oven to 325°F. Set a kettle of water to boil. With an electric mixer, beat cream cheese on medium speed until light and fluffy, 2 to 3 minutes. Add remaining 1¼ cups sugar in a slow, steady stream. Beat in salt and vanilla. Add eggs, one at a time, beating until just combined after each addition and scraping down sides of bowl as needed (do not overmix). Place springform pan in a large, shallow roasting pan. Pour filling into crust. Dollop cranberry sauce, 1 teaspoon at a time, over filling; swirl sauce into filling with a skewer or toothpick.

**4.** Transfer roasting pan to oven. Carefully pour enough boiling water into roasting pan to come halfway up sides of springform pan. Bake until cake is set but still slightly wobbly in center, about 1 hour 15 minutes.

**5.** Carefully transfer pan to a wire rack to cool completely. Refrigerate, uncovered, 6 hours, or loosely covered, up to 1 day. To serve, run a knife around edges of cake and unmold cheesecake onto a platter.

# Pumpkin Snacking Cake

## SERVES 12 TO 16

*When you have a house full of guests around Thanksgiving, bake a snacking cake—pumpkin flavored, of course—to have on hand. Cream cheese frosting pairs beautifully, but you could also just keep it supersimple with a sprinkling of cinnamon-sugar (mix ½ teaspoon cinnamon and ¼ cup sugar).*

Unsalted butter, for pan

1½ cups unbleached all-purpose flour, plus more for pan

1½ cups sugar

1 teaspoon baking powder

½ teaspoon baking soda

1½ teaspoons ground cinnamon

¾ teaspoon ground ginger

½ teaspoon ground nutmeg

⅛ teaspoon ground cloves

⅛ teaspoon ground allspice

½ teaspoon kosher salt

1 can (15 ounces) pumpkin purée

4 large eggs, room temperature

½ cup safflower oil

Cream Cheese Frosting (page 240; see headnote)

½ cup coarsely chopped walnuts, toasted (optional; see tip)

**1.** Preheat oven to 350°F. Butter a 9-by-13-inch baking pan. Dust with flour, tapping out any excess. In a medium bowl, whisk together flour, sugar, baking powder, baking soda, cinnamon, ginger, nutmeg, cloves, allspice, and salt.

**2.** In a large bowl, whisk together pumpkin purée, eggs, and oil. Fold flour mixture into pumpkin mixture until well combined. (The batter should be thick and smooth.) Pour batter evenly into prepared pan, smoothing top with an offset spatula.

**3.** Bake until golden brown and a cake tester comes out clean, 30 to 35 minutes. Transfer pan to a wire rack to cool 15 minutes. Turn out cake onto rack to cool completely.

**4.** Transfer to a serving platter. Spread frosting evenly over cooled cake with an offset spatula. Sprinkle with chopped walnuts and set out for snacking.

**BAKING TIP**

While the cake is
cooling, you can
toast the chopped
walnuts: Place in
a single layer on
a rimmed baking
sheet and bake
in the already
preheated 350°F
oven until fragrant,
about 6 minutes.

**DECORATING TIP**

Use almond paste
to form stems
for raspberry
mushrooms and
acorn caps for
chestnuts.

# Holiday Yule Log

MAKES ONE 8-INCH LAYER CAKE

*We turned the traditional bûche de Noël on its head, to resemble a playful stump. No fancy piping is required: You create the bark-like effect simply by pulling an offset spatula through the frosting vertically and swirling the top.*

## FOR THE CAKE

1½ sticks (¾ cup) unsalted butter, room temperature, plus more

1½ cups unbleached all-purpose flour, plus more

2 teaspoons baking powder

1¼ teaspoons kosher salt

2 cups peeled roasted chestnuts

2 tablespoons golden rum

1 cup packed light-brown sugar

¾ cup granulated sugar

1 tablespoon vanilla extract

5 large eggs, separated, room temperature

## FOR THE FROSTING

4 sticks (2 cups) unsalted butter, room temperature

5 cups confectioners' sugar

1 teaspoon vanilla extract

Pinch of kosher salt

2 cups peeled roasted chestnuts

3 tablespoons golden rum

4 ounces bittersweet chocolate (61 to 70% cacao), melted and cooled

2 tablespoons unsweetened Dutch-process cocoa powder

Garnishes (see tip)

**1. Make the cake:** Preheat oven to 375°F. Butter three 8-inch round cake pans. Line bottoms with parchment; butter parchment. Dust with flour, tapping out any excess. In a medium bowl, whisk together flour, baking powder, and salt.

**2.** In a food processor, purée chestnuts with rum and 2 tablespoons water. Add both sugars; process to combine. Add butter and vanilla; process to combine. Add egg yolks; process to combine. Transfer chestnut mixture to a large bowl; whisk in flour mixture. In a separate large bowl, whip egg whites with an electric mixer until soft peaks form. Fold into batter.

**3.** Divide batter among pans; smooth tops with an offset spatula. Bake until a cake tester comes out clean, 20 to 25 minutes. Transfer pans to a wire rack to cool 10 minutes. Turn out cakes onto rack to cool completely.

**4. Make the frosting:** With an electric mixer on medium-high speed, beat butter until pale and creamy, about 2 minutes. Add confectioners' sugar, ½ cup at a time, beating well after each addition and scraping down sides of bowl as needed. Beat in vanilla and salt. Divide mixture evenly between 2 bowls.

**5.** Purée chestnuts and rum in food processor until almost smooth; stir into a bowl of frosting. (If frosting looks slightly broken, chill, then whisk to combine.) Stir melted chocolate and cocoa into other bowl of frosting.

**6.** Place a cake layer on a cake turntable or stand. Spread ¾ cup chestnut frosting on top of first cake layer. Repeat with second layer and another ¾ cup chestnut frosting. Top with final layer. Coat top and sides with 1 cup chestnut frosting. Refrigerate 30 minutes. Coat cake with chocolate frosting, then decorate by pulling a small offset spatula through the frosting and swirling the top. Refrigerate at least 30 minutes and up to 3 days. Bring to room temperature before garnishing as desired and serving.

# Pavlova Wreath

### SERVES 10

*This stunner of a dessert could actually be one of the simplest things to come out of your kitchen this holiday season. Whip up some meringue and pipe it with a large or star tip into individual-serving-size puffs to form a wreath shape, bake, then top it with a tangy yogurt-cream and bright in-season fruit.*

6 large egg whites, room temperature

2 cups and 1 tablespoon sugar, plus more for rolling

1 teaspoon distilled white vinegar

1 teaspoon cornstarch

1 teaspoon vanilla extract

1½ cups fresh or partially thawed frozen cranberries

1¼ cups full-fat skyr or Greek yogurt

½ cup heavy cream

Pomegranate seeds, red currants, and mint leaves, for serving

**1.** Preheat oven to 250°F. Trace a 10-inch circle on a piece of parchment with a pencil. Trace a 5½-inch circle in center of larger circle. Place on a baking sheet, tracing-side down.

**2.** In a large bowl, with an electric mixer, whisk egg whites on medium-high speed until soft peaks form. Gradually add 1½ cups sugar, beating until stiff peaks form. Beat in vinegar, cornstarch, and vanilla.

**3.** Transfer mixture to a large pastry bag fitted with a large plain tip (such as Ateco #808). Pipe 10 evenly spaced mounds (each about 2¼ inches in diameter and 2 inches high) onto parchment in a circle, using traced ring as a guide. With the back of a spoon, create a hollow in each mound. Bake until ring easily lifts off parchment, about 1 hour 10 minutes. Turn off heat (do not open oven door); leave in oven 1 hour.

**4.** In a small saucepan, bring ½ cup sugar and ½ cup water to a boil. Add cranberries; return to a boil, then reduce to a simmer and cook about 2 minutes. Remove from heat and let cool in liquid. Drain cranberries and transfer to a wire rack; let dry about 30 minutes. Roll 3 tablespoons of individual berries in remaining sugar to coat.

**5.** In a medium bowl, whisk skyr with heavy cream and remaining 1 tablespoon sugar until silky; divide equally between hollows in pavlovas. Garnish with both sugared and unsugared cranberries, pomegranate seeds, currants, and mint.

**SERVING TIP**

Change up the fruit,
with fresh berries
or citrus, depending
on the season or
holiday.

# 7
# Baking Basics

*Every baker needs a repertoire of dependable cake recipes, delicious frostings and fillings, and fanciful garnishes. Turn the pages to discover your new trusted favorites.*

———

# Mix-and-Match Cakes

*Mix and match the basic cake recipes that follow with your favorite frostings (pages 237–242). Use the Basic Chocolate Cake as the base for the Faux-Stone Cake (page 22) and Spring Nest Cake (page 196), or swap out the Watercolor Cake's white layers (page 41) for tender lemon ones. Your delicious options are limitless.*

---

**Each recipe yields one of the following:**

Three 8-inch round layers  /  Two 9-inch round layers  /  One 9-by-13-inch sheet  /  3 to 4 dozen cupcakes

## Classic White Cake

3 sticks (1½ cups) unsalted butter, room temperature, plus more for pans

3 cups cake flour (not self–rising), plus more for pans

2 teaspoons baking powder

1 teaspoon kosher salt

½ teaspoon vanilla extract

1 cup whole milk

2¼ cups sugar

8 large egg whites, room temperature

**1.** Preheat oven to 350°F. Butter cake pans; line with parchment. Butter parchment; dust with flour, tapping out any excess. For cupcakes, line muffin tins with paper liners.

**2.** In a medium bowl, whisk together flour, baking powder, and salt. In a small bowl, stir vanilla into milk. With an electric mixer on medium speed, beat butter until smooth, about 2 minutes. With machine running, gradually add 2 cups sugar; beat until pale and fluffy, 3 to 5 minutes. Reduce speed to low. Add flour mixture in three batches, alternating with milk mixture and beginning and ending with flour. Beat until just combined (do not overmix).

**3.** In a clean large bowl, beat egg whites on medium speed until foamy, about 3 minutes. Gradually add remaining ¼ cup sugar; beat on high speed until stiff, glossy peaks form, about 4 minutes. Gently fold egg whites into batter in three additions.

**4.** Divide batter evenly between prepared pans, smoothing tops with an offset spatula. Bake until tops spring back when pressed and a cake tester comes out clean (see suggested time below). Transfer pans to a wire rack to cool 15 minutes. Turn out cakes or cupcakes onto rack to cool completely.

**8-inch round layers: about 25 minutes; 9-inch round layers: 25 to 30 minutes; 9-by-13-inch cake: 45 to 50 minutes; cupcakes: about 18 minutes**

# Yellow Butter Cake

3 sticks (1½ cups)
unsalted butter,
room temperature,
plus more for pans

4 cups cake flour
(not self-rising),
plus more for pans

1 tablespoon
baking powder

¼ teaspoon kosher salt

3 cups sugar

1 tablespoon
vanilla extract

6 large eggs, room
temperature

1½ cups whole milk

**1.** Preheat oven to 350°F. Butter cake pans; line with parchment. Butter parchment; dust with flour, tapping out any excess. For cupcakes, line muffin tins with paper liners.

**2.** Sift together flour, baking powder, and salt into a medium bowl. With an electric mixer on medium speed, beat butter and sugar until pale and fluffy, 3 to 5 minutes. Add vanilla, then add eggs, one at a time, beating well after each addition and scraping down sides of bowl as needed.

**3.** With mixer on low speed, add flour mixture in three batches, alternating with milk and beginning and ending with flour. Scrape bottom of bowl; mix until smooth.

**4.** Divide batter evenly between prepared pans, smoothing tops with an offset spatula. Bake until a cake tester comes out clean (see suggested time below). Transfer pans to a wire rack to cool 15 minutes. Turn out cakes or cupcakes onto rack to cool completely.

8-inch round layers: about 40 minutes; 9-inch round layers: 50 to 55 minutes; 9-by-13-inch cake: 60 to 65 minutes; cupcakes: 20 to 22 minutes

# Tender Lemon Cake

2½ sticks (1¼ cups)
unsalted butter,
room temperature,
plus more for pans

3¾ cups unbleached
all-purpose flour,
plus more for pan

1 tablespoon
plus ¾ teaspoon
baking powder

¾ teaspoon kosher salt

2½ cups sugar

5 large eggs,
room temperature

Finely grated
zest of 1½ lemons

1¼ teaspoons
vanilla extract

1¼ cups buttermilk

**1.** Preheat oven to 325°F. Butter cake pans; line with parchment. Butter parchment; dust with flour, tapping out any excess. For cupcakes, line muffin tins with paper liners.

**2.** In a medium bowl, whisk flour, baking powder, and salt. With an electric mixer on medium speed, beat butter and sugar until pale and fluffy, 3 to 5 minutes. Add eggs, one at a time, beating well after each addition and scraping down sides of bowl as needed. Mix in zest and vanilla.

**3.** With mixer on low speed, add flour mixture in three batches, alternating with buttermilk and beginning and ending with flour.

**4.** Divide batter evenly between prepared pans, smoothing tops with an offset spatula. Bake until golden brown and a cake tester comes out clean (see suggested time below). Transfer pans to a wire rack to cool 15 minutes. Turn out cakes or cupcakes onto rack to cool completely.

8-inch round layers: 40 to 45 minutes; 9-inch round layers: about 50 minutes; 9-by-13-inch cake: 60 to 65 minutes; cupcakes: about 25 minutes

# Basic Chocolate Cake

3 sticks (1½ cups) unsalted butter, room temperature, plus more for pans

¾ cup unsweetened Dutch-process cocoa powder, plus more for pans

½ cup boiling water

3 cups cake flour (not self-rising)

1 teaspoon baking soda

½ teaspoon kosher salt

2¼ cups sugar

1 tablespoon vanilla extract

4 large eggs, lightly beaten

1 cup whole milk

**1.** Preheat oven to 350°F. Butter cake pans; line with parchment. Butter parchment; dust with cocoa, tapping out any excess. For cupcakes, line muffin tins with paper liners.

**2.** In a small bowl, stir together cocoa and the boiling water until a smooth paste forms; let cool. In a medium bowl, whisk together flour, baking soda, and salt.

**3.** With an electric mixer on medium speed, beat butter and sugar until pale and fluffy, 3 to 5 minutes. Mix in vanilla. Add eggs in a slow stream, mixing until incorporated.

**4.** Gradually whisk milk into cocoa paste. With mixer on low speed, gradually add both flour and cocoa mixtures to butter mixture.

**5.** Divide batter evenly between prepared pans, smoothing tops with an offset spatula. Bake until a cake tester comes out clean (see suggested time below). Transfer pans to a wire rack to cool 10 minutes. Turn out cakes or cupcakes onto rack to cool completely.

8-inch round layers: 35 to 40 minutes; 9-inch round layers: 50 to 55 minutes; 9-by-13-inch cake: 45 to 50 minutes; cupcakes: about 25 minutes

# One-Bowl Chocolate Cake

Unsalted butter, for pans

1½ cups unsweetened Dutch-process cocoa powder, plus more for pans

3 cups unbleached all-purpose flour

3 cups sugar

1 tablespoon baking soda

1½ teaspoons baking powder

1½ teaspoons kosher salt

3 large eggs, room temperature

1½ cups warm water

1½ cups buttermilk

¾ cup safflower oil

1½ teaspoons vanilla extract

**1.** Preheat oven to 350°F. Butter cake pans; line with parchment. Butter parchment; dust with cocoa, tapping out any excess. For cupcakes, line muffin tins with paper liners.

**2.** In a medium bowl, whisk together cocoa, flour, sugar, baking soda, baking powder, and salt. Add eggs, the warm water, buttermilk, oil, and vanilla. With an electric mixer on low speed, whisk until smooth, about 3 minutes.

**3.** Divide batter evenly between prepared pans. Bake until a cake tester comes out clean (see suggested time below). Transfer pans to a wire rack to cool 20 minutes. Turn out cakes or cupcakes onto rack to cool completely.

8-inch round layers: 35 to 40 minutes; 9-inch round layers: 50 to 55 minutes; 9-by-13-inch cake: about 75 minutes; cupcakes: 20 to 25 minutes

# Mix-and-Match Fillings

*Lemon, passionfruit, cranberry—these add a brightness to desserts that we at Martha can't get enough of: Use the citrus-mousse filling between the tender lemon layers on page 26. The versatile curds play into both cakes (pages 68 and 74) and cupcakes (page 178); you can make them up to 5 days in advance.*

## Citrus Mousse Filling

MAKES ABOUT 5½ CUPS

1¼ teaspoons unflavored gelatin

2 tablespoons cold water

1¼ cups granulated sugar

1 tablespoon finely grated lime zest plus ¼ cup fresh juice (from 2 limes)

7 large egg yolks plus 2 egg whites

½ cup fresh lemon juice (from 2 to 3 lemons)

¼ teaspoon kosher salt

1 stick (½ cup) plus 2 tablespoons unsalted butter, cut into ½-inch pieces

1 cup heavy cream

3 tablespoons confectioners' sugar, sifted

**1.** In a small bowl, sprinkle gelatin over cold water. Let stand until softened, about 5 minutes. Meanwhile, in a medium saucepan, whisk together 1 cup granulated sugar, the zest, and egg yolks. Whisk in lime and lemon juices and salt. Add butter and cook over medium-high heat, whisking constantly, until butter melts and mixture is thick enough to coat the back of a spoon, about 5 minutes. Stir in gelatin mixture; cook until completely dissolved, about 1 minute more.

**2.** Pour curd through a fine-mesh sieve into a nonreactive bowl. Press plastic wrap directly on surface of curd; refrigerate until cold, about 1 hour (or stir over an ice bath until chilled, about 15 minutes).

**3.** Whisk cream with confectioners' sugar until stiff peaks form. Whisk curd briefly to loosen, then fold in whipped cream. With an electric mixer, whisk egg whites until soft peaks form, then gradually beat in remaining ¼ cup granulated sugar until stiff peaks form. Gently fold into curd mixture. Refrigerate in an airtight container at least 1 hour and up to 2 days.

# Passionfruit Curd

MAKES ABOUT 2 CUPS

1 cup sugar

½ cup passionfruit purée

6 large egg yolks, lightly beaten

6 tablespoons unsalted butter, cut into pieces

**1.** In a medium saucepan, combine sugar and passionfruit purée; bring to a rapid simmer over medium-high heat.

**2.** Meanwhile, lightly beat egg yolks in a medium bowl. Slowly whisk ¼ cup passionfruit mixture into eggs. Transfer mixture back to saucepan, whisking constantly. Cook until mixture thickens and coats the back of a spoon, 2 to 4 minutes.

**3.** Strain mixture through a fine-mesh sieve into a heatproof bowl. Whisk in butter, a few pieces at a time, until completely incorporated. Press plastic wrap directly on surface of curd, then refrigerate until cold, at least 2 hours and up to 5 days.

# Coconut Lemon Curd

MAKES ABOUT 2½ CUPS

1 cup sweetened shredded coconut

1 cup sugar

1 tablespoon cornstarch

1 teaspoon finely grated lemon zest plus ½ cup fresh juice (from 2 to 3 lemons)

1 teaspoon finely grated Meyer lemon zest, plus ¼ cup fresh juice (from 1 to 2 lemons)

½ teaspoon kosher salt

8 large egg yolks

1 stick (½ cup) plus 2 tablespoons unsalted butter, cut into pieces

**1.** Preheat oven to 350°F. Spread coconut in an even layer on a baking sheet and bake until dry but not golden, about 10 minutes. Let cool.

**2.** In a medium saucepan, whisk together sugar, cornstarch, both zests, and salt. Whisk in egg yolks, then both lemon juices. Add butter and cook over medium heat, whisking constantly, until butter melts, mixture is thick enough to coat the back of a spoon, and bubbles are forming in center of pan, about 5 minutes.

**3.** Strain mixture through a medium-mesh sieve into a bowl, pressing on solids to remove as much liquid as possible; discard solids. Press plastic wrap directly on surface of curd, then refrigerate until very firm and cold, at least 2 hours and up to 3 days. Before using, whisk to loosen, then stir in coconut.

# Cranberry Curd

MAKES ABOUT 2½ CUPS

12 ounces fresh or frozen cranberries (3 cups)

¾ cup sugar

⅔ cup fresh orange juice (from 2 large oranges)

¼ teaspoon kosher salt

6 tablespoons unsalted butter, room temperature

1 large egg plus 2 large egg yolks

**1.** In a medium saucepan over medium heat, combine cranberries, sugar, orange juice, and salt. Simmer until cranberries burst and collapse, about 10 minutes. Remove from heat; stir in butter until melted. Strain mixture through a medium-mesh sieve into a bowl, pressing on solids to remove as much liquid as possible; discard solids.

**2.** In another bowl, whisk together egg and yolks. Slowly whisk 1 cup cranberry mixture into egg mixture; return to saucepan along with remaining cranberry mixture and cook over medium-low heat, stirring occasionally, until thickened and coats the back of a spoon, about 6 minutes. Press plastic wrap directly on surface of curd, then refrigerate until cold, at least 2 hours and up to 5 days.

# Orange Curd

MAKES ABOUT 2½ CUPS

1 cup sugar

1 tablespoon grated orange zest plus ½ cup fresh orange juice

1 teaspoon grated lemon zest plus 2 tablespoons fresh lemon juice

8 egg yolks, room temperature

¼ teaspoon kosher salt

1 stick (½ cup) plus 2 tablespoons unsalted butter, cut into ½-inch pieces

**1.** In a medium saucepan, whisk together sugar, both zests, and egg yolks. Whisk in both juices and salt. Add butter and cook over medium-high heat, whisking constantly, until butter melts and mixture is thick enough to coat the back of a spoon, about 5 minutes (do not boil).

**2.** Remove pan from heat while continuing to whisk. Pour curd through a fine-mesh sieve into a heatproof bowl. Press plastic wrap directly on surface of curd, then refrigerate until cold, at least 2 hours and up to 5 days.

# How to Fill a Pastry Bag

*Pastry bags and tips are sold separately and together in sets. Begin with a basic set and add as your decorating skills advance. Disposable bags are sold in bulk but consider resusable ones if you're an avid baker. Whatever you decide, the first step is to prepare a pastry bag properly.*

## 1. Snip the end of the bag:

Snip off the pointed end of a pastry bag—enough to accommodate the base of the coupler. Insert the coupler base into the pastry bag, making sure the screw threads are covered. (Alternatively, you can first insert the coupler base into the bag to help determine how much of the end to snip off.)

## 2. Add the tip:

Place your desired tip over the base of the coupler. Twist on the outer ring to secure the tip in place. Whenever you want to change tips—but use the same color frosting—simply unscrew the outer ring.

## 3. Fill the bag with frosting:

To fill the bag with frosting, hold the bag with one hand. Fold the top over into a cuff around your hand. Fill the bag only halfway to prevent overflow when piping. Unfold the bag and push the frosting toward the tip to get rid of any air bubbles. Twist the bag closed, and, if desired, secure with a binder clip or rubber band. If you're using multiple colors, fill all your bags before you get started. Set each bag in a tall glass while you work.

## 4. Pipe the design:

To pipe, hold the pastry bag firmly near the top with your dominant hand, using your other hand to guide the bag. Follow the piping steps, squeezing the frosting toward the tip. Adjust pressure as needed, depending on the design.

**DECORATING TIP**

**If frosting starts to get too runny, refrigerate it briefly—just until firm but not long enough to harden.**

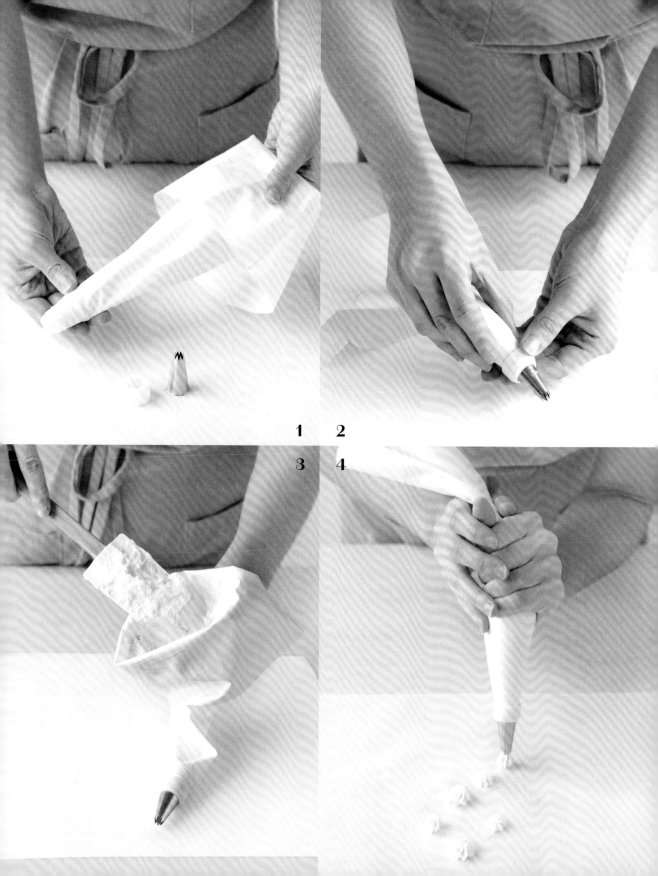

**1**

**2**

**3**

**4**

# Mix-and-Match Frostings

*Here are our favorite frostings for the best swoops and swirls.*
*When decorating a cake, you'll generally need 1 to 2 cups of frosting for the top,*
*1 to 1½ cups between layers, and the remainder around the sides.*

---

## Swiss Meringue Frosting

MAKES ABOUT 5 CUPS

5 large egg whites, room temperature

1¼ cups sugar

¼ teaspoon cream of tartar

¾ teaspoon vanilla extract

Combine egg whites, sugar, and cream of tartar in a heatproof bowl set over (not in) a pot of simmering water. Whisk constantly until whites are warm to the touch and sugar is dissolved, 2 to 3 minutes. (Test by rubbing mixture between your fingers; it should feel completely smooth.)

## Swiss Meringue Buttercream

MAKES ABOUT 5 CUPS

5 large egg whites, room temperature

1¼ cups sugar

Pinch of kosher salt

4 sticks (2 cups) unsalted butter, cut into tablespoons, room temperature

1½ teaspoons vanilla extract

**1.** In the bowl of a stand mixer, combine egg whites, sugar, and salt. Set bowl over (not in) a pot of simmering water and whisk until warm to the touch and sugar is dissolved, 2 to 3 minutes. (Test by rubbing mixture between your fingers; it should feel completely smooth.)

**2.** Transfer to a stand mixer fitted with the whisk attachment. Starting on low speed and gradually increasing to medium-high during the first minute, beat mixture to stiff, glossy peaks, 7 to 10 minutes.

**3.** Reduce speed to medium-low and add butter, 2 tablespoons at a time, beating well after each addition. (Don't worry if buttercream appears curdled after butter has been added; it will become smooth again with continued beating.) Add vanilla and beat just until combined. Switch to paddle attachment and beat buttercream on low speed, 2 minutes, to remove any air bubbles.

**Note: For recipes requiring 6 to 8 cups Swiss Meringue Buttercream, simply add an additional egg white and ¼ cup sugar.**

## Chocolate Swiss Meringue Buttercream

MAKES 6¼ CUPS

1¼ cups sugar

5 large egg whites, room temperature

Pinch of kosher salt

3 sticks (1½ cups) unsalted butter, cut into tablespoons, room temperature

9 ounces bittersweet chocolate (61 to 70% cacao), melted and cooled

**1.** In a large heatproof bowl, combine sugar, egg whites, and salt. Set bowl over (not in) a pot of simmering water and whisk until warm to the touch and sugar is dissolved, 2 to 3 minutes. (Test by rubbing mixture between your fingers; it should feel completely smooth.)

**2.** Remove bowl from heat. With an electric mixer, whisk on high speed until cool (test by touching bottom of bowl), 7 to 10 minutes. Change to the paddle attachment; with mixer on medium-high speed, add butter, 2 tablespoons at a time, until combined. Beat in chocolate.

### TINTING FROSTING

**1. Choose your colors.** We prefer gel-paste food colorings (like those made by Americolor), which are more concentrated than liquid varieties.

**2. Divide your frosting into bowls,** reserving some plain frosting in case you need to lighten a color.

**3. Using a toothpick or wooden skewer,** add the gel one drop at a time, stirring with a flexible spatula to combine. Remember that the color will darken over time.

## Italian Meringue Buttercream

MAKES ABOUT 4½ CUPS

1¼ cups sugar

5 large egg whites, room temperature

Pinch of cream of tartar

4 sticks (2 cups) cold unsalted butter, cut into pieces

1 teaspoon vanilla extract

**1.** In a small saucepan over medium heat, bring sugar and ⅔ cup water to a boil. Continue boiling until syrup registers 238°F (soft-ball stage) on a candy thermometer.

**2.** With an electric mixer, whisk egg whites on low speed until foamy. Add cream of tartar, increase speed to medium-high speed, and beat until stiff but not dry; do not overbeat.

**3.** With mixer on high speed, add sugar syrup to egg whites in a stream, beating about 3 minutes. Add butter, piece by piece, beating until spreadable, 3 to 5 minutes; beat in vanilla. (If icing curdles, keep beating until smooth.)

## Seven-Minute Frosting

MAKES ABOUT 3 CUPS

2 large egg whites

⅔ cup sugar

½ teaspoon cream of tartar

2 tablespoons light corn syrup

¼ cup cold water

In a large heatproof mixing bowl, combine egg whites, sugar, cream of tartar, corn syrup, and cold water. Set bowl over (not in) a pot of simmering water; with an electric mixer on high speed, beat until glossy, stiff peaks form, about 5 minutes. Remove bowl from heat; continue beating on high until mixture is no longer warm to the touch, about 5 minutes more.

# Vanilla Buttercream

MAKES 4 CUPS

3 sticks unsalted butter, room temperature

½ teaspoon vanilla extract

1 pound confectioners' sugar, sifted (4 cups)

2 tablespoons whole milk

Pinch of kosher salt

With an electric mixer, beat butter on medium-high speed until pale and creamy, about 2 minutes. Reduce speed to medium and add confectioners' sugar ½ cup at a time, beating after each addition and scraping down sides of bowl as needed. Add vanilla, milk, and salt and beat until buttercream is smooth.

# Strawberry Buttercream

MAKES ABOUT 5 CUPS

4 large egg whites, room temperature

1¼ cups sugar

3 sticks (1½ cups) unsalted butter, cut into small pieces, room temperature

1½ cups fresh strawberries, puréed

**1.** In a heatproof bowl set over (not in) a pot of simmering water, combine egg whites and sugar. Whisk until sugar dissolves and mixture registers 160°F on a candy thermometer.

**2.** With an electric mixer on medium speed, whisk mixture for 5 minutes. Increase speed to medium-high and whisk until stiff, glossy peaks form, about 6 minutes. Reduce speed to medium and add butter, one piece at a time, whisking well after each addition.

**3.** With mixer on low, add strawberry purée, and beat until smooth, 3 to 5 minutes.

# Coconut Buttercream

MAKES ABOUT 4 CUPS

5 large egg whites, room temperature

1 cup sugar

¼ teaspoon kosher salt

6 tablespoons raw unrefined coconut oil (3 ounces), room temperature (solid)

3 sticks (1½ cups) unsalted butter, room temperature, cut into small pieces

**1.** In a heatproof bowl set over (not in) a pot of simmering water, combine egg whites, sugar, and salt. Whisk constantly until sugar dissolves and mixture is warm and feels completely smooth when rubbed between fingertips. Remove bowl from heat. With an electric mixer, starting on low speed and gradually increasing to medium-high, whisk until stiff, glossy peaks form, about 2 minutes. Continue whisking until bottom of bowl is cool to the touch, about 10 minutes more.

**2.** Reduce speed to medium-low and whisk in coconut oil, a few tablespoons at a time, then butter, a few pieces a time, until combined, scraping down sides of bowl as needed. Switch to paddle attachment and beat on low speed until smooth, about 1 minute more.

**HOW TO FIX BROKEN BUTTERCREAM**

**If your frosting starts to break (looks curdled or soupy), increase the speed of the mixer and continue for one to three minutes more.**

# Cream Cheese Frosting

3 sticks (1½ cups) unsalted butter, room temperature

3 packages (8 ounces each) cream cheese, room temperature

4 cups confectioners' sugar, sifted

1 tablespoon vanilla extract (optional)

Pinch of kosher salt

With an electric mixer on medium-high speed, beat butter until smooth, about 2 minutes. Add cream cheese and beat until fluffy. Reduce speed to low and add confectioners' sugar, ½ cup at a time. Add vanilla, if using, and salt, and mix until smooth and well combined, scraping down sides of bowl as needed.

# Citrus Cream Cheese Frosting

2 packages (8 ounces each) cream cheese, room temperature

1 stick (½ cup) unsalted butter, room temperature

1 pound confectioners' sugar, sifted (4 cups)

2 teaspoons freshly grated citrus zest plus 4 teaspoons juice

With an electric mixer on medium-high speed, beat cream cheese until smooth, about 2 minutes. Add butter and sugar; beat until smooth, about 5 minutes. Beat in zest and juice until combined.

# Chocolate Frosting

2¼ cups confectioners' sugar, sifted

¼ cup unsweetened Dutch-process cocoa powder

Pinch of kosher salt

6 ounces cream cheese, room temperature

1½ sticks (¾ cup) unsalted butter, room temperature

9 ounces bittersweet chocolate (61 to 70% cacao), melted and cooled

¾ cup crème fraîche or sour cream

In a medium bowl, sift together confectioners' sugar, cocoa, and salt. In a separate medium bowl, beat cream cheese and butter with an electric mixer on medium-high speed until smooth. Reduce speed to medium-low; gradually add cocoa mixture and beat until combined. Pour in chocolate in a slow, steady stream. Add crème fraîche; beat until thoroughly incorporated.

# White Chocolate Frosting

2 packages (8 ounces each) cream cheese, room temperature

9 ounces white chocolate, coarsely chopped (1¾ cups), melted and cooled slightly

2½ sticks (1¼ cups) unsalted butter, room temperature

2 tablespoons fresh lemon juice

1¼ cups confectioners' sugar, sifted

With an electric mixer on medium-high speed, beat cream cheese until smooth, about 2 minutes. Add chocolate and beat until smooth, scraping down sides of bowl as needed. Add butter and lemon juice; beat to combine. Reduce speed to low and add confectioners' sugar, ¼ cup at a time, until well blended.

# Double Chocolate Frosting

MAKES ABOUT 4 CUPS

¼ cup unsweetened Dutch-process cocoa powder

¼ cup boiling water

2 sticks (1 cup) unsalted butter, room temperature

¼ cup plus 2 tablespoons confectioners' sugar, sifted

Pinch of kosher salt

12 ounces bittersweet chocolate (70% cacao), melted and cooled

In a small heatproof bowl, whisk together cocoa and boiling water until cocoa is dissolved. With an electric mixer, beat butter, confectioners' sugar, and salt on medium-high speed until pale and fluffy, 3 to 5 minutes. Reduce speed to low; add melted and cooled chocolate and beat until combined, scraping down sides of bowl as needed. Add cocoa mixture and beat until completely smooth. (Frosting can be stored in refrigerator up to 5 days; bring to room temperature and beat before using.)

# Whipped Ganache Frosting

MAKES ABOUT 2 CUPS

8 ounces best-quality semisweet, bittersweet, or milk chocolate, coarsely chopped (1½ cups)

1 cup heavy cream

⅛ teaspoon kosher salt

Place chocolate in a medium heatproof bowl. In a medium saucepan, bring cream just to a boil. Pour over chocolate and add salt; let stand 10 minutes. Whisk until chocolate is melted and mixture is smooth and shiny. Let cool at room temperature, stirring until thickened, 45 to 60 minutes. With an electric mixer on medium-high speed, beat until fluffy, 2 to 4 minutes. Use immediately.

# Chocolate Ganache Glaze

MAKES ABOUT 1½ CUPS

8 ounces best-quality semisweet, bittersweet, or milk chocolate, coarsely chopped (1½ cups)

¾ cup heavy cream

2 tablespoons light corn syrup

Place chocolate in a medium heatproof bowl. In a medium saucepan, bring cream and corn syrup just to a boil, stirring to combine. Pour over chocolate; let stand 10 minutes. Whisk until chocolate is melted and mixture is smooth and shiny. Use immediately.

# Chocolate Ganache

MAKES ABOUT 3 CUPS

16 ounces best-quality semisweet, bittersweet, or milk chocolate, coarsely chopped (3 cups)

2 cups heavy cream

Place chocolate in a large heatproof bowl. In a small saucepan, heat cream until simmering and pour over chopped chocolate; let stand 10 minutes. Stir until combined. Set aside about one hour, stirring occasionally. (If not using immediately, press plastic wrap directly onto surface until ready to use.)

**STORAGE TIP**

**If you'll be using buttercream within several hours after making it, cover the bowl with plastic wrap, and set it aside at room temperature. Otherwise, transfer the frosting to an airtight container and store it in the refrigerator up to 3 days.**

# White Chocolate Ganache

MAKES ABOUT 2½ CUPS

12 ounces white chocolate, coarsely chopped

1 cup heavy cream

Place chocolate in a medium heatproof bowl. Heat cream in a small saucepan over medium heat just until simmering; pour over chocolate. Let stand 5 minutes, then stir gently with a spatula until fully incorporated. Cover and refrigerate until set but still spreadable, about 1 hour. (If ganache is too firm, let stand at room temperature or beat in an electric mixer until softened.)

# Caramel Sauce

MAKES ABOUT 1 CUP

1 cup sugar

¼ teaspoon kosher salt

½ cup heavy cream

½ teaspoon vanilla extract

**1.** In a small saucepan, stir together sugar, salt, and ¼ cup water. Heat over medium, stirring occasionally, until sugar dissolves and syrup is clear. Cook, without stirring but washing down sides of pan with a wet pastry brush a few times to prevent crystals from forming, until syrup comes to a boil. Continue to cook, gently swirling pan occasionally, until syrup is dark amber, 8 to 10 minutes.

**2.** Remove pan from heat; carefully pour in cream (it will bubble). Stir in vanilla until smooth. Let cool completely. (Sauce can be refrigerated in an airtight container up to 2 weeks; reheat in microwave or a small pot before serving.)

# Vanilla-Bean Milk Frosting

MAKES ABOUT 3 CUPS

¼ cup unbleached all-purpose flour

1 cup whole milk

1 teaspoon vanilla extract

Pinch of kosher salt

2 sticks (1 cup) unsalted butter, room temperature

1 cup sugar

1 vanilla bean, split and seeds scraped

**1.** In a small saucepan, whisk together flour, milk, vanilla extract, and salt until smooth. Heat over medium-high, whisking constantly, until mixture becomes thick and resembles pudding, 3 to 4 minutes. Transfer to a bowl; cover with plastic wrap, pressing it directly on surface, and cool completely, about 30 minutes.

**2.** With an electric mixer, beat butter, sugar, and vanilla seeds on medium speed, scraping down sides of bowl as needed, until light and fluffy, about 2 minutes. Add cooled milk mixture and continue to beat until frosting looks like whipped cream, 2 to 3 minutes. Use immediately.

# Whipped Cream

MAKES ABOUT 6 CUPS

3 cups heavy cream

1 cup sugar

¼ teaspoon kosher salt

1 tablespoon vanilla extract

Combine cream, sugar, salt, and vanilla in the bowl of a stand mixer fitted with the whisk attachment. Mix on low speed until sugar is dissolved, about 1 minute. Increase speed to medium-high and whisk to firm peaks, about 3 minutes more.

# Garnishes and Extras

*Colored sprinkles, sugared citrus, glittering cranberries—*
*these are the finishing touches that catch one's eye. All of these can be made*
*ahead of time and added right before serving.*

## Homemade Sprinkles

MAKES 1¼ CUPS

1½ cups confectioners' sugar, sifted

1 tablespoon light corn syrup

¼ teaspoon vanilla extract

Gel–paste food coloring in pink, peach, and fuchsia

**1.** In a small bowl, combine sugar, 2 tablespoons water, the corn syrup, and vanilla. Stir until mixture has consistency of glue, adding more water, if necessary, ¼ teaspoon at a time. Divide evenly into 3 small bowls; tint with gels, one drop at a time, until desired color is achieved.

**2.** Transfer lightest-colored mixture to a pastry bag fitted with a small pastry tip (such as Ateco #2). Pipe long, thin lines onto parchment-lined baking sheets. Fill pastry bag with medium-colored mixture; repeat piping. Fill pastry bag with darkest-colored mixture; repeat piping. Let stand, uncovered, until very firm, at least overnight. Once lines are dry, break enough into small pieces for ⅓ cup; keep remaining sprinkles long for garnish.

## Candied Citrus Slices

MAKES 12

1 large lemon or orange

1 cup sugar

**1.** Prepare an ice-water bath; set aside. Using a mandoline or sharp knife, cut fruit into 12 paper-thin slices; discard seeds and ends of rind.

**2.** Bring a medium saucepan of water to a rolling boil. Remove from heat and add fruit slices; stir until softened, about 1 minute; drain. Immediately plunge slices into ice-water bath; drain.

**3.** Bring sugar and 1 cup water to a boil in a medium skillet, swirling to dissolve sugar. When liquid is clear and bubbling, reduce heat to medium-low. Add fruit slices, arranging them in one layer with tongs. Simmer (do not boil) until rinds are translucent, about 1 hour.

**4.** Transfer fruit slices to a parchment-lined baking sheet. Let stand until ready to serve. Citrus slices can be stored in an airtight container at room temperature up to 1 day.

# Fresh Ricotta

MAKES 2¾ CUPS

½ gallon (8 cups) best–quality whole milk

1½ cups best–quality heavy cream

1 teaspoon kosher salt

¼ cup fresh lemon juice (from 2 lemons), strained to remove pulp

**1.** Combine milk, cream, and salt in a 4- to 5-quart pot, and warm mixture over medium-high heat, stirring frequently with a wooden spoon to prevent scorching, until mixture registers 195°F on a candy thermometer, about 15 minutes.

**2.** Add lemon juice, gently stirring until just combined. Remove pot from heat and let stand 5 minutes. The combination of the acid and the residual heat in the mixture will cause it to coagulate or curdle—separating into a soft mass (curds) and a cloudy liquid (whey).

**3.** After lining a mesh colander with a triple layer of cheesecloth and placing it inside a deeper, slightly larger bowl, gently pour curds and whey into colander. Let mixture stand, pouring off whey occasionally, until most whey drains from still-wet curds, about 20 minutes.

**4.** Gather up ricotta in cheesecloth and turn it out into a bowl. Serve within a few hours, or refrigerate up to 4 days. For a denser ricotta, which can be preferable for baking, hang it to drain for another hour. Repurpose whey or discard it.

# Sugared Cranberries

MAKES 2 CUPS

2 cups sugar

2 cups fresh or partially thawed frozen cranberries

¾ cup superfine sugar

**1.** In a small saucepan, bring sugar and water to a simmer over medium heat, stirring until sugar dissolves. Remove from heat and let cool 10 minutes. Place cranberries in a medium bowl; pour syrup over cranberries. Let cool completely. Wrap with plastic and refrigerate overnight.

**2.** Drain cranberries in a colander over a bowl, reserving syrup for another use. Place superfine sugar in a shallow dish. Add cranberries in batches, rolling to coat with sugar. Spread sugared cranberries in a single layer on a baking sheet; let stand at room temperature until dry, about 1 hour.

# Chocolate curls

Using an offset spatula, spread melted chocolate in an even layer on the back of a rimmed baking sheet; let stand until set. Holding a bench scraper at a 45-degree angle, scrape the chocolate into curls. For a fast and simple method, use a vegetable peeler: Shave curls from a bar of chocolate right over the cake.

# Acknowledgments

This book began with the Martha Stewart team whipping up Swiss meringue, baking cake layers, and testing new decorating techniques—and went to press during COVID-19, when shelves were cleared of flour and we were socially distancing. During this time, more than ever, baking became a way of nurturing our families, friends, and even ourselves. We hope, with this book, you continue to find comfort and joy in baking.

Special thanks to the team who made this book happen: editorial director Susanne Ruppert, who led the charge, with the invaluable help of Nanette Maxim, Laura Wallis, and Sanaë Lemoine. Standing ovation for art director Michael McCormick, who masterminded the beauty on each page. Photographer Lennart Weibull, with the help of digital technician Lorie Reilly, captured the inviting images that grace these pages. (For a full list of the talented photographers, see page 248.) Ensuring every photo looked both delicious and beautiful were art director James Dunlinson and prop stylist Megan Hedgpeth, along with the gracious Anne Eastman. Food stylists Molly Wenk and Caitlin Haught Brown discovered new and wonderful ways for you to fall in love with cake. Assisting them were two of the most hardworking and delightful bakers, Shannon Feulner and Jeanette Zepeda-Dalbey. Heartfelt thanks to our friends and colleagues at MSL, for endless inspiration and guidance. For your unwavering support, thank you to Marquee Brands, especially Kevin Sharkey, Thomas Joseph, Kavita Thirupuvanam, Kim Dumer, and Carolyn D'Angelo. Thank you to our Clarkson Potter family, who asked us to do this book as a follow-up to *Martha Stewart's Cookie Perfection,* namely Jennifer Sit, Jennifer Wang, Terry Deal, Kim Tyner, Lydia O'Brien, Marysarah Quinn, Stephanie Huntwork, Aaron Wehner, Doris Cooper, Kate Tyler, Stephanie Davis, and Jana Branson. Finally, thank you to all the essential workers who kept the wheels in motion.

# Photography Credits

All photographs by Lennart Weibull with the following exceptions:

Sidney Bensimon: Pages 114, 122

Aya Bracket: Page 59

Chris Court: Page 110

Ren Fuller: Page 178

Bryan Gardner: Pages 16, 117, 134, 233

Julia Gartland: Page 222

Raymond Hom: Page 71

John Kernick: Page 181

Mike Krautter: Pages 39, 50, 113, 177

Ryan Liebe: Pages 11, 42, 56, 151

Kate Mathis: Page 205

James Merell: Page 206

Johnny Miller: Pages 5, 6, 9, 60, 99, 227, 230, 236, 243

Marcus Nilsson: Pages 32, 36, 118, 125

Ngoc Minh Ngo: Pages 26, 65, 67, 75, 86, 155

Paolo + Murray: Page 126

Con Poulos: Page 189

Armando Rafael: Pages 133, 198

Anson Smart: Page 85

Alpha Smoot: Pages 130, 141, 142, 156, 160, 164

Yuki Sugiura: Pages 15, 19, 176

Romulo Yanes: Page 106

Justin Walker: Page 217

# Index

Note: Page references in *italics* indicate photographs.

# On the Cover

*For the cover, we made the Chocolate-and-Vanilla Zebra Cake on page 45 with an extra layer, covered it with a glossy chocolate frosting, chilled it, then poured a silky dark chocolate ganache over the top for added decadence.*